Brenda

Seven Years in the
Life of a Child

Sylvia Boomsma

NEWMAN SPRINGS PUBLISHING
320 Broad Street
Red Bank, NJ 07701

First originally published by Newman Springs Publishing 2020

ISBN 978-1-64801-385-0 (Paperback)
ISBN 978-1-64801-386-7 (Digital)

Printed in the United States of America

This book is dedicated to my dad,
Rev. Henry M. DeRooy,
who taught me to write and to think,
and assured me back when I couldn't write a
book about our crazy, marvelous life
(because I was too busy living it):
"Even if you never write a book, your life is a book,
and—trust me—people are reading it."

Preface

They hate to forget a scrap of the past.
It is all hoarded up and, if they live long enough,
some of the ordinary things that have
happened to them this week will end up as epics.
Experiences have to turn into tales,
and this process takes a long time.
—Schoolmaster Hugh Hambling
(*Akenfield, Portrait of an English Village* by Ronald Blythe)

When our children were young, Bob and I always had our worst annual fight in December. We were both writers. We had met as English majors in college. After we married, our home was probably the only one in town with two copies of *The Oxford English Dictionary*; neither of us would part with our cherished volumes.

But to get back to our worst annual fight… Every December, I would write a Christmas letter for our family and friends, filling it with humorous vignettes of our family's life. My letter was always too long and too detailed. Every December, Bob asked to read my letter before it was printed. Every December, he told me it was too long and too detailed. With cross-outs, rewrites, and notes in the margin, he reminded me that my stories did not recount the way things had actually happened. He went about this in the kindest possible way, approaching me with apologies and disclaimers, all the while knowing that by bedtime we would no longer be on speaking terms.

The experiences I recount here are things that happened in our day-to-day life many years ago. Some of my stories may be too long and too detailed. Perhaps I've embellished a bit here and there. I'm sure my memories differ slightly from my children's and from

Bob's, were he here to take a red pen to my epic. In any case, these experiences are extraordinary—more than I realized at the time—because Brenda is not, and never has been, ordinary. Even if every detail were accurate, you would still find Brenda's story anything but commonplace.

Chapter 1

When I smiled at them, they scarcely believed it;
the light of my face was precious to them.

—Job 29:24

When we had dislodged enough bureaucratic logjams to believe that our foster child Brenda could really, finally, legally become our daughter, we sat her down and asked her what she wanted to be called. Her birth mother had given her the first name Brenda, and that's what we had been calling her for the years we had known her. Only after she had lived in our home for several months did we learn that in her birth family, she was called by her middle name, Evelyn, to distinguish her from an adult half sister also named Brenda.

The meaning of names mattered to me, and I had pondered over which of her two names suited her better. The name Evelyn, meaning "light and life," was apt, for no child ever radiated more bright energy, warmth, or interest in other people. No one could hold a more determined optimism or live with greater exuberance. The name Brenda, which means "firebrand," seemed equally fitting for a child who had passed through the flames of adversity and carried away embers of buoyancy and hope which inspired others to face their own troubles with courage.

Of course, she was not burdened by the significance of names. Like any nine-year-old, she would simply choose the name she liked best. We posed our question: Which name did she prefer, Brenda or Evelyn? She considered for several moments, deep in thought. At last, she spoke.

"Can I be called Michelle?" she asked hopefully.

That was our Brenda. Independent. Sprightly. Always a step ahead, working the angles, making the most of every opportunity.

"No," we answered.

By this time, our lives had become so entwined with Brenda's that it felt as if we had always known her. It was inconceivable—but true—that on the day of her calamity, I was completely ignorant of anything amiss. The screech of brakes was far away; I did not hear the thud or Brenda's cries of pain. Of any day's multifarious tragedies, we know only a little about a very few. They happen to strangers in faraway places and generally have little effect on the rest of the world. But sometimes, one tragic moment has long tendrils that reach into other lives in unexpected ways—even into the lives of people who didn't know anything bad had happened.

On March 30, 1996, a little girl walked along a dusty road in the Caribbean resort town of Trujillo, Honduras. More likely, she skipped and danced because that's the kind of girl she was and because it was her birthday, the day she turned five years old. As she twirled playfully, a breeze caught the piece of paper she carried, and it floated into the road. Without a thought, Brenda danced after it, light on her bare feet. And then one of those moments happened.

In our home, the day passed without incident. On March 30, 1996, our family was adjusting to the departure of Elías, a five-year-old foster child from Nicaragua who had gone home the day before, after a five-month stay. I was not distracted from my tasks that spring afternoon. While life and death contended for the remnants of Brenda, I washed little boys' clothes, reattached wheels to cars and heads to dolls, and comforted our four daughters as they wandered around the house getting used to the empty places Elías had left.

It was almost a year before a tendril of Brenda's misfortune reached into our lives. One day in February 1997, my husband, Bob, answered a phone call from an acquaintance, Dr. Jim Schumaker, a family practice physician in Wisconsin. He was just back from Trujillo, where, during a short-term mission trip, his medical team had discovered Brenda. The doctor believed she was a candidate for the Madison chapter of Healing the Children, an organization that provided free foster and medical care to children who came to the

States without their parents to receive life-saving treatments that were not available to them in their home countries. This kind of specialized foster care is what we used to do in our spare time. "Pretty weird hobby, Bean," Bob would sometimes say to me, shaking his head. But he was completely devoted to every foster child who entered our home. He could no more turn down a child in need than I could. So we usually had a family of eight: two parents, two birth children, two adopted children, and two foster children. The long-term foster child already with us was a severely impaired six-year-old boy from the Philippines named Noli. That left one empty bed in our three-bedroom ranch home, but it was never empty for long, because there was always a child in need of Madison's state-of-the-art medical care, and that child would also need a family to love and care for her during her time away from home.

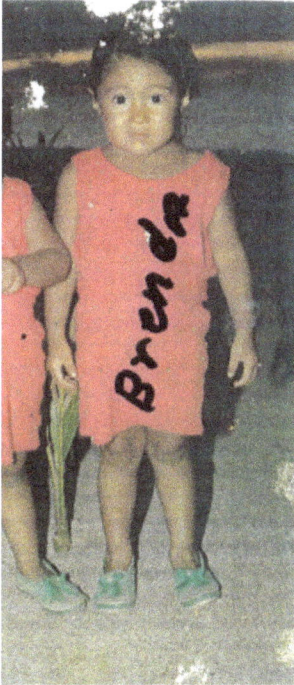

Brenda prior to
her accident

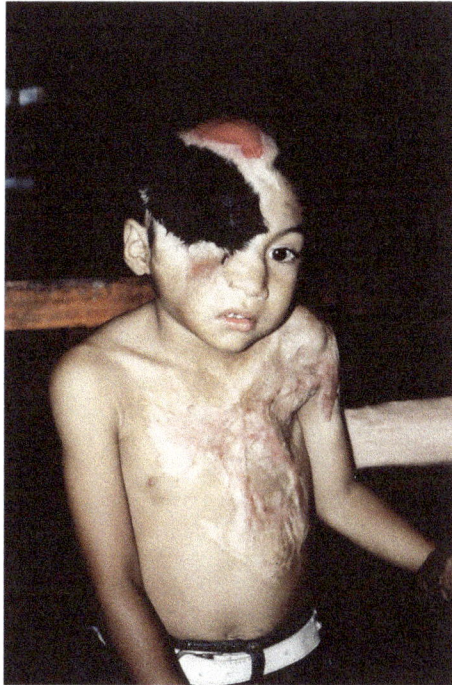

Brenda as we first saw her

Dr. Schumaker described five-year-old Brenda, who had been struck by a delivery truck which crushed her skull and dragged her along the road, stripping the flesh from her chest, abdomen, and shoulder. Miraculously, she had survived her critical injuries. However, even after several surgeries, she was badly disfigured, with a dented forehead, one eye, a swatch of hairy scalp covering a quarter of her face, and a raw, perpetually weeping bald spot on the top of her head. Dr. Schumaker described her bluntly as "the Quasimodo of her village." Yet, undaunted, the lively Brenda had made friends with every Gringo on Dr. Schumaker's visiting medical team—not as a patient but as the flirtatious and charming beggar she was, flitting among them with an astonishing and indomitable *joi de vivre*.

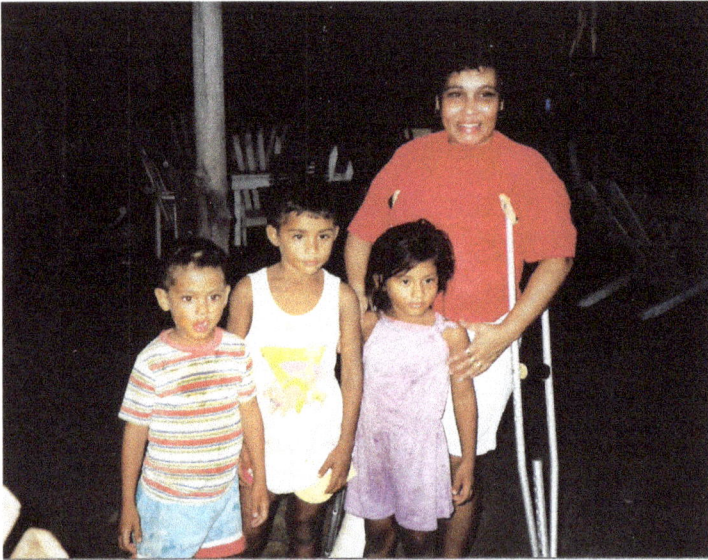

Brenda's mother, twin sister, and nephews in Trujillo

Soon Madison's Healing the Children community was abuzz with the story of Brenda. Because we had provided foster care to other children who had undergone extensive facial surgeries, we were unofficially designated Madison's craniofacial family. We agreed to host Brenda, and I figured we'd take it all in stride; nothing could surprise us after the cases we'd seen. But I was not prepared for the snapshot of Brenda which soon arrived in the mail. As we sat around the table after supper that evening, I pulled out the photo, and silence fell. Fourteen-year-old Grace winced and stared quietly at the picture before passing it to twelve-year-old Laura. "This is worse than I thought," Laura whispered, handing the photo to her eleven-year-old sister, Kate. Kate's face was sad for a moment and then brightened. "Look, Mom!" she exclaimed. "She has a heart on her chest, like Raggedy Ann." I looked more closely at the photo and saw for myself, in the hills and valleys of road-burned and grafted skin, the pattern of a small heart. How fitting for a human rag doll, a torn-up girl who had been patched together as well as she could be with the scraps left by her accident.

As I tucked eight-year-old Rose into bed that night, she asked where Brenda would sleep. Since Rose was the only one whose double bed had an empty space, I gave the obvious answer: "Well, probably here with you."

Rose was thoughtful, her face troubled. "Do you think she'll sleep *toward* me or *away* from me?" she asked.

I took her hand in my own. "Remember, Rose," I said, "once you get to know the person inside, you'll hardly notice the outside." Rose knew from experience the truth of my prediction, yet she still looked anxious as I turned out the light and left the room.

By the time we received word of Brenda's arrival date, our daughters' initial shock had turned to pity and from pity to excited anticipation. Bob and I left home a little after 6 p.m. that Friday evening, to arrive at O'Hare Airport by 9 p.m., Brenda's arrival time. Held up a bit by heavy rains and thunderstorms and feeling pressed, we scurried into the terminal just in time to learn that Brenda's plane was not expected for three hours. Finally, a few minutes before midnight, the plane landed, and a sleepy Brenda emerged with her chaperon, Bruce. Shy and subdued, she clung to Bruce's hand until the last possible moment and then transferred to Bob and me without tears. When we arrived home in the early morning hours, I helped Brenda change into a nightgown and tucked her into bed beside Rose. She was so obedient I thought she would walk off a cliff if I asked her to. *This'll be a piece of cake*, I thought.

Brenda's first weekend in our home

The next day, the well-rested Brenda emerged. High-spirited and self-assured, she was soon running the house—especially her foster sisters who were falling all over each other in their desire to welcome her and fulfill all her wishes, which were spoken in Spanish with the winsome confidence of a wastrel whose stock-in-trade was the American tourist. That day, she began calling Bob and me Dad and Mom and adopted our family as her own without a backward glance. Not once did she cry tears of homesickness. Curious and fearless, she wanted to try everything. At festivals we happened to attend on her first Saturday and Sunday, she insisted on having her face—or what remained of it—painted. That same weekend, she learned to ride a bike with training wheels and went swimming in our aboveground pool. She was never tentative about trying new foods. She asked for a serving from each dish and declared that she loved them all. Though one side of her jaw had been crushed in the accident and she could not open her mouth or chew, she had a way of pushing food past her locked teeth with her thumb and then swallowing everything without chewing it. She could eat even steak, if it was cut into small pieces. She received correction with good humor as we briefed her on American house rules. For example, we don't run on the kitchen table or throw litter out the car window, and when we've had half a glass of water, we don't pour the other half out on the floor with a splash.

Brenda's arrival marked the end of the lazy, hazy days of summer, even though it was only June. Between soccer practice, basketball camp, piano lessons, and errands, we fit in almost-daily visits to some doctor or other. The two surgeons Brenda saw within days of her arrival were more circumspect than I had hoped, as they examined her with deep concern and talked about the challenges of this multifaceted case. Dr. Hardy, a pediatric craniofacial reconstruction surgeon at the University of Wisconsin Hospital, seemed to be in a quandary about the best way to proceed—as if he needed to go home and sleep on it, preferably for several nights. His habit was to think out loud while examining the patient and manipulating the pertinent parts of her body. Shall he proceed with more skin grafts, like those done in Honduras? Or should he start the long and complicated process of expanding the skin she already had, stretching it to meet the need?

I encouraged him to do whatever he felt was best, regardless of the time factor. "And by the way," I asked as casually as I could, "what sort of a timetable are we on?"

"Hmmm," he responded, gazing at Brenda as she scribbled in a coloring book. "I'm thinking she should be ready for an eye prosthesis in about a year."

My heart sank. A whole year?! I was beginning to realize that my dreams of a nearly perfect outcome within six months were unrealistic. Dr. Hardy explained that the loss of an eye and its surrounding structures is a real misfortune because it's impossible to reconstruct eyelids, lashes, ducts, and other delicate, functional parts. I left our first appointment discouraged. I had expected the surgeons to have a plan and be upbeat—after all, they had seen pictures of Brenda in advance and should have known what they were up against. Yet I appreciated their honesty; they did not hide their apprehension or instill false optimism about her prognosis.

Brenda took the appointments in stride. To her, medical examinations were little more than an annoying interruption in her fun new American life. Dr. Wood, a plastic surgeon, got out his camera, stood Brenda in front of a swatch of dark velvet, and took a series of photos, asking her in Spanish to turn this way or that, look up or down. When, at our next appointment, Dr. Hardy's camera and dark cloth appeared, Brenda was most cooperative, posing as she had for Dr. Wood but without cues, looking left, right, up and down. Completely unselfconscious, she was flattered that these Gringos wanted to take her picture.

When Dr. Hardy ordered a scan, his staff arranged for intravenous sedation: conventional wisdom would suggest that a lively six-year-old should be sedated since she must lie completely still for the duration of the test. However, knowing from experience that IV sedation can turn a painless twenty-minute test into an all-day hospital visit, I opted to take a chance on the wide-awake method. I was confident that with proper preparation by Child Psychologist Sylvia Boomsma, Brenda would be able to hold completely still. When I described, in Spanish, the test and the huge machine, she seemed quite accepting and not at all afraid. The day of the scan, we arrived on time, but the radiology department was running behind. No problem. My children were experts at killing time in waiting rooms. After thumbing through magazines and finding every underwear ad or picture of people kissing, my daughters and Brenda were well into a severe case of the sillies, and I was beginning to think Brenda's scan was a lost cause. When her turn arrived, I took her hand as she and I followed the white-coated technician down the long hallway. Inwardly dreading the day we would have to return to repeat the test under sedation, I explained to the fidgeting Brenda that she must lie completely still, as we had discussed at home. As the technician placed her head in the cradle and taped several Velcro straps across her forehead and body, she looked at me apprehensively. Perhaps she was beginning to doubt my promise that it would not hurt, *"ni un poquito"* (not even a little).

When in doubt, try bribery. "If you hold completely still for the test, I'll give you some candy," Child Psychologist Sylvia Boomsma whispered in Spanish into the anxious Brenda's ear. Brenda nodded, the technician excused me, and I walked back down that long corridor certain I had made a mistake in turning down sedation. Ten minutes later, the technician's assistant summoned me. "Is something wrong?" I asked, certain that the restless Brenda needed coaching in Spanish. But as we entered the room, the technician announced, "We're finished!" There lay Brenda, almost asleep and completely still, as she had been since I left. Of course, she received my praises—and the promised candy. Child psychologists *always* deliver on their bribes.

That evening at the supper table, we got into a discussion of our varying fluencies in Spanish. That's a sugarcoated way of saying the girls were having a heated argument about who knew the most Spanish words. To distract them from their increasingly fervent debate, Bob said, "Well, I don't know much Spanish, but I bet I know more English words than any of you."

Kate looked at him doubtfully. "Oh yeah?" she challenged. "Do you know what *Lilliputian* means?" She settled back with a look of triumph on her face.

"Yes," Bob answered, casually buttering a roll. "It means 'very small.'"

Kate's initial surprise gave way to suspicion. Her eyes narrowed. "Have you been reading my *American Girl* magazine?" she asked.

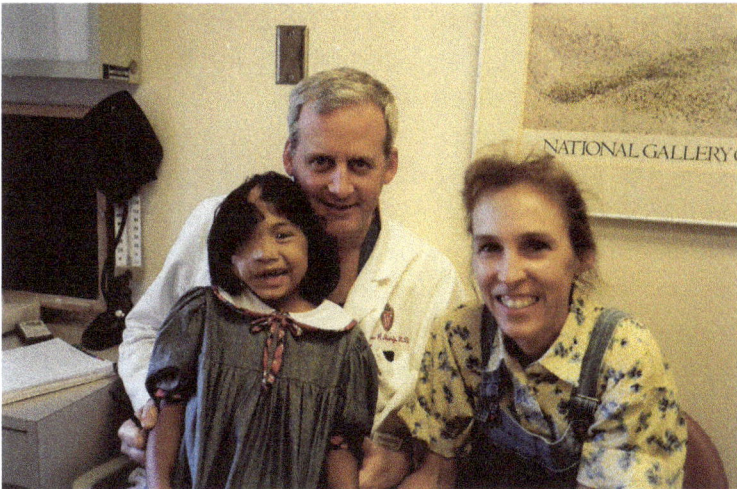

Brenda, Sylvia, and Dr. Hardy

The next Monday morning, Brenda's first preoperative odyssey began at the University of Wisconsin Hospital. When we arrived at the registration desk, a receptionist handed me a flowchart directing us to our next five stops. After Brenda's tour of pediatrics and visits to the lab, anesthesia, admissions, and insurance, we arrived at the surgery clinic for our appointment with Dr. Hardy, who would be Brenda's chief surgeon and the architect of her facial remodel. He arrived with a cortege of student doctors, a phenomenon we were to observe often during Brenda's months under Dr. Hardy's care. As the students watched, he measured Brenda's head and described the surgery. These white-coated followers never said a word to him or to us; apparently theirs was not to question or comment but only to listen and observe. When Dr. Hardy was called away to the phone in the hallway, his entourage flowed from the room, presumably to eavesdrop and perchance gain some crumbs of knowledge from his end of the conversation. After three examinations and four attempts at urine collection, Brenda's appointments were finally finished. We climbed wearily into the car and headed home to a late lunch.

Such were the distractions that stalled a landscaping project I had begun in the backyard: terracing part of the hill behind our house and making a patio. Saturday dawned warm and sunny, and I looked forward to spending most of the afternoon rearranging soil and rocks. The terracing I had done so far and the rock wall I had built were the cause of much head shaking on Bob's part. When he had earlier surveyed my rock retaining wall and declared it unstable, I had torn it down and prepared to try again. I refused his help, even though some large rocks were so heavy I could barely move them. On that Saturday, as I rolled an especially large boulder into place, it slipped, smashing the tip of my left middle finger. Gasping, I pulled off my glove and watched blood seep from the nail bed. Nearly doubled over with pain, I staggered to the kitchen, holding my dripping finger. As Bob looked up in horror, I squeaked out (much to his relief, I'm sure), "I smashed my finger with a big rock." My finger felt like it was on fire, and I could not hold back tears as the pain shot through my hand.

After washing and bandaging my finger, I walked to the window and noticed Bob once again standing before my wall, scratching his head in dismay. Deciding to put my wall-building career to an abrupt end, he dismantled the entire structure and rebuilt a much safer and more attractive one. He must have moved a couple tons of stone as he worked the rest of the afternoon. Later on, I thanked him for finishing my task and comforting me after my injury.

"How is your finger now?" he asked.

"Much better," I replied, holding it up for inspection. "But I won't be able to drive for a while."

"Why not?" he asked, puzzled.

"Because my birdie finger is injured," I answered with a chuckle.

While Bob worked outdoors, I supervised the girls, who had moved indoors for a game of dress-ups. We had a vast collection of lacy, frilly dresses from thrift stores, in various sizes. The idea of putting on such attire for play mystified Brenda, so I told her in Spanish that when girls play dress-ups, they wear pretty clothes and pretend to be grand, rich ladies. Her face lit up with glee. She bounced down the hall and reappeared moments later, all ruffles and lace, with a couple pounds of costume jewelry tinkling as she waltzed along. "*Yo soy rica!*" (I'm rich!) the little waif crowed.

Installing a small patio is a big job, but Bob faithfully persevered with the project I had started. After building a wall far superior to mine, he purchased and laid down pea gravel and patio stones. Twenty hours, untold tons, and four hundred dollars later, I'm sure he rued the day he had ever let a woman start such a task. Meanwhile, Dr. Hardy was busy with deconstruction and reconstruction on a smaller scale. His first foray into Brenda's head—a projected three-hour operation—turned into six hours of tedium. The scarring around her crushed jaw was so extensive that most of her molars were encased in scar tissue. A dysfunctional metal jaw joint had to be meticulously extracted from layers of bone, muscle, and soft tissue that had grown over it. To complete his operation, Dr. Hardy placed two tissue expanders under Brenda's scalp. These were like plastic bags, which were empty when he put them in place. Over the course of several weeks, he would regularly inject fluid into each expander so that, like growing water balloons under her skin, they would stretch her scalp and force new skin to grow. This was a painful process, and Brenda complained more about her scalp than about her jaw, where Dr. Hardy had done all that digging.

The long days of Brenda's hospitalization provided time for me to think about the future: a year of surgeries, procedures, and therapy; several months of injections; and the fact that Brenda would look worse before she looked better. When she was discharged and we returned home, I realized that housekeeping would need to drop a few points on my priority list. Simply maintaining a right-of-way in the common areas became my new standard. Recalling that the previous summer I had established an effective system for shared housework, I dug around until I found the chore chart I had made. Predictably, it was greeted with moans and groans. However, the ever-optimistic Kate asked me hopefully what the girls would get for doing their chores. "You get to keep living here," I answered wearily. Her expression told me that *that* was a dubious reward indeed.

Yet our daughters made willing sacrifices daily. Their summer project was to get Brenda through her surgeries and make life as pleasant for her as possible. When she wanted a big sister to play outdoors with her, one of the girls would lay her book aside and take her to the neighborhood park. When she was too ill to play outdoors, one of them would read to her or help her assemble a jigsaw puzzle. When she was in pain, they would pull out a board game to distract her. In spite of occasional lapses, they were, overall, so selfless that I longed to give them that coveted trip to Disneyworld that they talked about every spring. Yet I knew in my heart that they would probably never see Disneyworld—or even Great America—with their dad and me. And I wondered, *What will their childhood memories be like?* I hoped and trusted that when they were old enough to look back and reflect, they would care more about their opportunities to touch and change the lives of little ones than about the extravagant family vacations they never had.

Chapter 2

As the weeks passed, the expanders in Brenda's scalp grew, and her head became more and more lumpy, like a bed pillow that had gone through the washing machine. Our friends gave her an assortment of hats, but one by one, her head outgrew them. Head pain was almost constant, and she found it hard to settle down at bedtime. Laying her head on her pillow was like resting on a water balloon, and no matter which way she turned, she could not get comfortable.

As her skin stretched and became thinner, the corner of an expander broke through, and the resulting perforation in her scalp enlarged with each injection. The clear plastic expander protruding through the healed edges of skin created the illusion that her head was giving birth to a sandwich bag full of water. Even at the university hospital, where abnormal is normal, Brenda's head was the object of stares and whispers; but she was—or had resolved to be—unaware that she was a curiosity to others. As he examined Brenda in the surgery clinic twice each week, Dr. Hardy would scratch his head and ponder aloud. In the end, he always ordered another injection to each expander to ensure that there would be enough new scalp to suit his blueprint for the next operation.

We often waited an hour or more to see the doctor. This did not faze my daughters, who were quite at home in waiting rooms and knew how to while away the time. I was surprised when they chose to go along on these weird family outings but also glad for their help and company. They always found ways to keep Brenda entertained while we waited in small examining rooms: perusing magazines to find boyfriends for each other; spinning each other on swiveling stools; drawing on chalkboards; or using shiny chrome doorknobs as convex mirrors to hilariously exaggerate facial contortions. The ride home usually included a postmortem on the examination or procedure Brenda had undergone, with a highly embellished account of her fear and pain. Such commiserating always ended with a pitch for ice cream to help (the oblivious) Brenda recover from her trauma.

Several weeks into the scalp expansion project, Brenda began complaining of head and stomach pain. Her eye swelled shut, and she ran fevers. Dr. Hardy immediately started antibiotics and ordered a hiatus from injections. After a few days, she was much improved, and the injections resumed. All seemed well until one evening after lights-out, when a clandestine wrestling match ended with shrieks from Brenda and calls of alarm from Kate. Apparently, an inadvertent kick had split part of the incision line covering the infected area on Brenda's scalp, releasing an impressive display of blood and serum. I made a series of phone calls and left messages, dialing with one hand and applying pressure to Brenda's seeping wound with the other. Though Dr. Hardy was in surgery, one of his assistants calmed my fears. Much to my relief, there would be no late-night visit to the emergency room. After calming Brenda, I attempted to rig a bandage with a knit headband and tucked her into bed. Of course, the bandage slipped off within a few hours, and by morning, an assortment of bodily fluids had stained her sheets and pillows.

One hot summer afternoon, I noticed that the house was unusually quiet as all the children were occupied with some enterprise in the basement. Even Noli had been carried down the stairs to participate in the mysterious project. Occasionally, one of the smaller, less conspicuous children passed through the kitchen on an errand, trying to appear nonchalant but stealing furtive glances my way as sheets, pillows, and sleepwear were smuggled to the basement half-concealed in their arms or under their shirts.

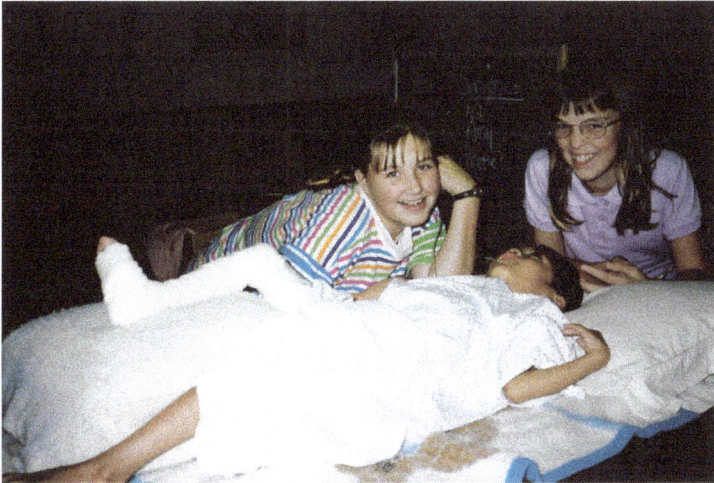

Nolita awaiting surgery

Finally feeling compelled to check on the activities, I descended the steps and found that our basement had been transformed into—of all things—a hospital. Sheets were hung from ceiling joists to separate patient rooms, a playroom, and a surgical suite. There lay the hapless Brenda on the operating table, draped in sheets and hooked up to IV tubing, which descended from the ceiling to her arm, where it was secured with what appeared to be half a roll of masking tape. Noli, now renamed Nolita, lay in a hospital gown with his/her legs wrapped in several yards of Ace bandage. Rose was in the next room, receiving an injection in one thigh while the other leg hung in a jury-rigged traction device. A chalkboard listed patients' names and locations, as well as the surgery schedule for the day. Capably in charge was the ever-efficient Grace, a fourteen-year-old who had long ago declared her aspiration to become a registered nurse.

Three aspects of this scene filled me with wonder. First, that all six children had managed to get along for a couple of hours without my intervention. Second, that these kids should choose to play hospital: as if they hadn't spent enough hours in medical establishments during the past month, they created a microcosm of the university hospital right in their own basement. Third, and of course always foremost in the mind of a mother, was the unspoken question, "Who's gonna clean up this mess?" I could see apprehension in the children's eyes as I discovered the destination of the many sheets, rolls of tape, bandages, and clothespins that had been absconded from their rightful places. They laughed with relief when I congratulated them on their creativity instead of (as I might have on some other day) reprimanding them for relocating seemingly a quarter of our worldly belongings. With a smile, I left them to their game. I would have to meet with the board of directors the next day to discuss the future of this hospital, but for today, they would have their fun. And I'd have a little quiet.

By the beginning of August, it was clear that there would not be any long vacation or camping trip this summer, because we had no respite care for Noli and Brenda's frequent appointments kept us on a short leash. Day trips worked well, however, and on one such outing, we found an old-fashioned amusement park in Green Bay where rides cost only ten to thirty cents apiece. Our $15-worth of tickets seemed like a well that would never run dry as the girls ran gleefully from one ride to another. Brenda's head pain was forgotten, and she was game for everything, but I forbade her to ride the bumper cars. As the older girls hopped into their *carritos*, I explained in Spanish to a tearful Brenda that the cars bump each other very hard, and I was worried that she might injure her head. "Please, Mom, *please*," she begged in English, with her most endearing expression. I was firm. She decided to try a different tactic. She turned to me with her arms crossed resolutely and a determined look on her face. "Well, in Trujillo," she announced in Spanish, "I ride bumper cars all the time, and my mama says it's perfectly *fine*."

As we progressed through the month of August, the intrepid Dr. Hardy was undaunted, even though some of the clinic staff questioned whether to continue injecting Brenda's extruded expander (in lay terms, the plastic bag sticking out of her head). "I don't think the skin around the extrusion can withstand any more expansion," a nurse declared to me, though I was sure she would never opine to Dr. Hardy with the same confidence. As Dr. Hardy gave the injection, the opening in Brenda's skin stretched and bled painfully but did not significantly tear.

In spite of her troubles, Brenda's spirits remained high; she was enjoying the great adventure of life in America. Her English vocabulary grew daily, and she began confusing her two languages. "*Como se llama* grass *en ingles?*" she might ask. ("How do you say *grass* in English?") "*Como se llama* gwater *in ingles?*" I tried to convince her that *water* (or, as she pronounced it, *gwater*) and *grass* are English words, but she refused to believe me.

Then she began to pose harder questions—the kind you know how to answer until someone asks you. What is water? What is the sky? Where do rocks come from? Why do dogs have tails? She was now past asking how you name common objects in English. She wanted to know what things were made of. Where they came from. Why they were there. It was clear that her accident had not damaged her intellect and her curious mind was ready for school. A few weeks before the fall semester was to begin, I took Brenda to the local elementary school to be registered and tested for English-as-a-Second-Language classes. She was at her charming, bright, affectionate best that day, confident and filled with excitement. While she chatted with the tester, I filled out enrollment forms in the same room. I watched as the tester, a vivacious young woman, showed her pictures of foods in order to see how many she could name in English. Brenda named several: *milk, hot dog, gwater*, and *chips*. The tester said enthusiastically, "Don't you just *love* chips?"

"Jyes!" Brenda answered emphatically. "I love chips!"

We walked down the hall to Brenda's classroom, where her teacher was preparing for the first day of school. Mrs. Brodersen, a grandmotherly woman with a kind face, hugged Brenda and welcomed her to the class. While we adults talked, Brenda wandered around exploring the classroom, marveling at the bright pictures and numerous books. When we were ready to leave, I thanked Mrs. Broderson and instructed Brenda to say goodbye.

"Goodbye, honey," Brenda said, reaching up to give Mrs. Brodersen a kiss.

Mrs. Brodersen, touched by Brenda's affection, hugged her tightly and said, "I love you, Brenda."

"I love *chips*!" Brenda answered.

First day of school, complete with scalp expanders

At-home mothers look forward to the beginning of the school year and the peace it brings to the house. But with children in four schools, including two in special education programs, it would take a few weeks to get the bugs out and adjust to our new routine. I delivered Brenda to her classroom on the first day and stayed with her until she felt comfortable and safe. That did not take long. Her classmates received her kindly, and the staff had made arrangements to provide an adult attendant the first couple of days. When I picked her up that afternoon, she looked weary and soon revealed her chief complaint about school. "Too hot," she said in English, with a weak voice and dramatic brow wiping. "I no like hot," she whined, as if she had not grown up in the tropics. Aside from the heat, she enjoyed her day and reported, in Spanish, that a nice lady had given her lunch in a restaurant (the cafeteria) and taken her to a park (the playground).

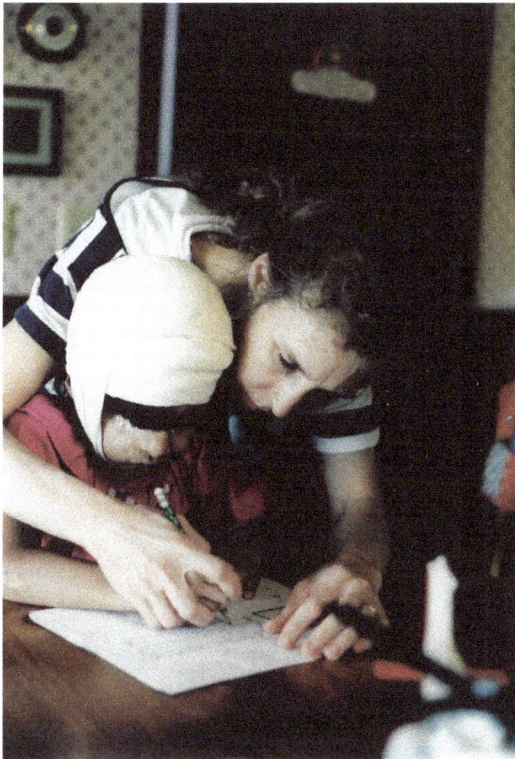

Practicing penmanship

Her second school day was interrupted by an injection appointment. When I picked her up shortly after lunchtime, she was carrying a silk flower which her nice lady had given her and which she planned to pass along to Kate, whose goldfish had recently died. In fact, this flower accompanied us throughout the afternoon until Brenda was able to deliver it, along with her condolences. While sitting in the surgery clinic waiting room, we happened to see my friend Linda, a nurse and a fellow Healing the Children foster mom. She was alarmed to see that another corner had emerged and Brenda's left expander was now exposed on both ends. "That can't be good," she said over and over, shaking her head. "I want you to tell the doctor that all your friends in the medical community are simply appalled at the condition of this child's head," she said adamantly.

I didn't report Linda's opinion to Dr. Hardy—not that I would have had time anyway. We went to an examining room promptly and then sat for an hour awaiting his arrival. I nervously watched the clock and periodically reminded the nurse that I had to leave at 2:40 to pick up my children at school. When 2:40 had arrived but Dr. Hardy had not, I took Brenda by the hand, went into the hall, announced to the nurse that we were leaving, and told her I would call later to find out when the doctor could *really* see Brenda. Suddenly three nurses began to scurry around, trying to find the doctor and insisting that we sit tight for just one more minute. Almost miraculously, Dr. Hardy appeared within seconds and proceeded to examine and inject Brenda while I called two schools to inform them that I would be running a bit late. The moral of the story: announce your departure while you still have fifteen minutes to spare.

Labor Day weekend promised to be a warm, dry, benevolent farewell to the summer season. That Friday evening, as we drove from Kate's soccer game to a restaurant for the team's weekly ice cream outing, Bob asked if I had a hooded sweatshirt or hat to cover Brenda's head. I did not. "Really, Bean," he warned, "someday someone's gonna look at that thing and heave."

Brenda and Kate enjoying a bike ride in the park

Early the next morning, Brenda reported to our bedside and announced that her head hurt and her hair was wet. The truth was that the right-side expander had emerged during the night and a mixture of blood and serum had been seeping from the new opening (the third) in her scalp. Though extruded expanders were becoming old hat at our house, Bob was disappointed and worried. It was a beautiful weekend; and the girls wanted to play outside, ride bikes, run through the sprinkler, go to the park, and otherwise enjoy summer's last hurrah. "What can we do?" I asked, "Make her sit on a chair all day?" So we let her go with a word of caution and a prayer that God would assign a few extra guardian angels. Meanwhile, Bob sealed the driveway while I began a round of Saturday morning chores. In the midmorning, Brenda approached me with a sad look on her face and a training wheel in her hand. "Something bad happened to my bike," she said.

"I'm certain Dad can fix it," I assured her, taking her hand and going off to look for our in-house Mr. Goodwrench.

Bob gathered his tools and had the training wheel installed within minutes. As Brenda took it for a test drive, Bob stood on the sidewalk holding his toolbox and looking pleased with himself. "Bob's Speedy Bike Repair," he said proudly. "We service training wheels while you wait."

Noli and Rose

Noli turned seven in October and promptly lost his first tooth the next day. We never found the tooth, but we all agreed that the gap in his mouth was the cutest thing we had ever seen. We oohed and aahed, and clapped our hands when Noli laughed in response. With his severe cognitive impairment, Noli had never reached developmental milestones at the "right" time—except for this lost tooth. So we celebrated thoroughly and made the most of his accomplishment. Brenda didn't appreciate our levity; she stood at a distance sulking. It was hard for the dethroned princess to step down and let someone else be the center of attention. She spent the rest of the day trying to rectify the situation by any tactic she could think of. She repeated every funny English phrase she knew. "You're so cute!" she told us all repeatedly in an exaggerated falsetto. When our laughter wore thin, she resorted to melodrama, exaggerating the smallest slights, jostles, and bumps. She complained at length, but not very convincingly, about head pain—generally a surefire way to get sympathy and concern. She pestered Bob until he spoke sharply to her and then pouted dramatically for half an hour. When the two had made amends, she apologized to him every five minutes for another half hour, rounding out her apologies with much drama and hand kissing. "I sorry, Daddy," she said in English. Each time Bob asked her what she was sorry for, she would answer, "I don't know, Daddy," laugh hysterically, and tug on his arm or leg.

Then she devised a most clever way to recapture the spotlight—by losing a tooth of her own. Finding that one of her teeth was a bit loose, she set to the business of hurrying Mother Nature along as diligently as she could. Every time I glanced her way, she was furiously wiggling that tooth. One afternoon she told me, in Spanish, that in Trujillo, when a child loses a tooth, she puts it under her pillow. During the night, a little *bruja* (witch) comes and replaces the tooth with money. I wondered how she knew of this tradition. How could a beggar child from a third-world country possibly wake to the thrill of coins underneath her pillow—if she even *had* a pillow? Had Brenda heard this story from an American? Indeed she had, and that American was Kate, who later mentioned to me that she had told Brenda about the Tooth Fairy. In spite of the language barrier, the pertinent fiscal details had been successfully communicated.

A few nights later, shortly after bedtime, Brenda emerged from her darkened bedroom triumphantly waving a bloody tooth in her hand. We all congratulated her and made much of the gap in her mouth. The little princess, happily ensconced once again in her rightful place, cheerily returned to bed with her tooth securely enclosed in an envelope addressed to the Tooth Fairy. Later on, Bob stealthily replaced the tooth with the loose change from his pockets. Of course, there was great celebration in the morning, and with expansive ceremony, Brenda gave each family member one of her coins.

Later I discovered to my dismay that Brenda had lain in the dark with her head over the side of the bed as blood dripped from her mouth into the carpet.

At last, the day of Brenda's surgery arrived. The preceding days had been strained: while Noli recovered from pneumonia followed by a bout of asthma and Bob left on a business trip, I prepared Brenda for another operation. Brenda was Dr. Hardy's last case of the day, and her surgery was delayed about six hours by someone else's emergency. When the doctor emerged from her operation at 10:30 p.m., he seemed more energetic after a fourteen-hour day in the operating room than I was after a few hours in the family waiting area. He was pleased with the operation and eager to describe what he had done. He pulled a ballpoint pen from the neck of his scrub shirt and glanced around for a piece of paper. Finding none within view, he put his foot on the edge of my chair and sketched an illustration of the procedure on the leg of his scrub pants.

A few hours later, before leaving for the night, Dr. Hardy stopped by Brenda's hospital room to see how she was doing. Finding her miserable with pain and nausea, he lay down on the bed beside her, speaking soothingly as he gently rubbed her back. The irritation I had felt while trying to distract an anxious Brenda through six hours of fasting and waiting earlier in the day was replaced by appreciation and admiration for this brilliant surgeon who was donating his time and expertise to give a little girl—a nobody in the eyes of some—a second chance at life.

I reminded myself of this often as we routinely waited an hour or two to see Dr. Hardy in the surgery clinic. Usually when we arrived for appointments, the doctor was delayed in surgery or simply running behind, or worse yet, no one knew where he was. During clinic hours, nurses directed him from room to room like the classic absentminded professor. During almost every appointment, Dr. Hardy asked me, "So how long can she stay?" Each time, I said, "That's up to you." Each time, he looked at her thoughtfully, mentally laying out his timetable. Each time, I reminded him that initially he had suggested a year. Each time, his eyes lit up. "A whole year?!" he would exclaim, as though I had just given him an unexpected gift. "I could do a *lot* in a year!"

As the days of Brenda's recovery passed, I realized that we had never set an appointment for suture removal. I called Sarah, Dr. Hardy's assistant, to see if she could fit us in during his clinic hours. "You'd better come in on Wednesday," Sarah suggested. "Be here before clinic starts at one o'clock. He's already got five patients scheduled at that time, but we'll squeeze you in somehow."

Fairly warned, we went to the clinic early, expecting the worst. One of the nurses told me that Dr. Hardy had forty-two patients to see that afternoon. We were the first to be called to an examining room, and as we walked down the long hallway behind the nurse, Dr. Hardy emerged from a staff room, muttering, "I don't know exactly where I'm supposed to go…"

"Follow the little girl in the pink shirt," I suggested, referring to Brenda, who was bouncing down the hallway in front of me. To my surprise, he did.

As he examined Brenda's scalp, his nurse kept him on track. "What day did I operate?" he asked. "And what is the date today?" He muttered to himself, deep in thought and assessment.

At last, he pronounced the incisions ready for suture removal and asked the nurse for the required instruments. At this point, Brenda correctly sized up the situation and made it clear that she had no intention of cooperating while others picked at her sensitive scalp. She started to squirm, the tears and sobs began, and I suggested that I remove her stitches at home.

"Have you ever removed stitches before?" the nurse asked.

"Too many times," I answered with a sigh.

"Great," she said with a smile, thinking of Dr. Hardy's next forty-one patients. She dropped the instruments into a plastic bag, handed it to me, and quickly ushered us from the examining room. Brenda fairly romped along as we left the building. The loveliness of a bright autumn afternoon was like an unexpected gift. We weren't sitting in a tiny cubicle marking off the dragging minutes! Just being outside in the sunshine and warm breezes seemed like something to celebrate.

Dr. Hardy was pleased with Brenda's progress. Ten days after the operation, she had almost completely recovered and returned to school, enjoying an expanderless existence, sleeping well, and selecting daily from her wardrobe of hats. Though the proportions of her head were back to normal, the benefits gained from all those weeks of injections, pain, and surgery seemed minimal to me. Bob echoed my sentiments when he saw her unbandaged head for the first time. "Um…what did Dr. Hardy do exactly?" he asked. His question reminded me that we were watching a meticulous process by which Brenda's appearance would be improved in increments. Dr. Hardy had already begun to talk about the next course of expander therapy, but he would give Brenda several weeks to recover before another operation, and this would provide a welcome hiatus from all those appointments and all that pain.

A week later, a freak October blizzard moved across the country, dumping three to four feet of snow out west. On Sunday, we got our piece of the action—three or four inches. The house suddenly felt warm and cozy, and the girls sipped hot chocolate as if it were a subzero winter day. As I gazed out the window at the beauty of the big flakes whirling through the air, I remembered Carolina, a seven-year-old foster child from Nicaragua who had been with us the previous winter. All through November, our children had talked of snow, but none had come. I tried to describe snow—*la nieva*—to a child from the tropics. "It covers the ground like a blanket—*una manta*," I told the incredulous Carolina in Spanish. Every morning after that, Carolina ran to the window to see if snow had come, and every morning she turned away disappointed. The day I awoke to see that a deep snow had fallen during the night, I soon heard Carolina's excited voice, piping from the bedroom, *"La manta! La manta!"* ("The blanket!") We could hardly keep her in the house long enough to eat breakfast. School was cancelled, and for our children, it was the snow day of all snow days, as they romped and played with a child who had never ridden on a sled or made even one snow angel.

A small hand on my arm called me back from my reverie that Sunday afternoon. Brenda's face was full of apprehension. "I want to go back to Trujillo," she told me gravely in Spanish. "I'm afraid of snow."

Chapter 3

O ne of the sad things about the Americanization of a third-world child is that she begins to view her former life through a first-world lens. This can happen within only a few weeks' time and the older the child, the more she is influenced by this dazzling new culture. Spoiled for life back in a hometown without malls, McDonalds, Barbies, or other American trappings, more than one foster child has asked us to adopt her. Many of our foster children, and their parents, have continued to correspond with us through the years. Almost inevitably, the requests begin—even asking us to buy the family a house or finance a child's college education. In the economy of our nation, the Boomsmas are middle class. But in the eyes of our foster children and their families, the Boomsmas have endless resources of wealth.

One November day when Brenda said, "I had five brothers and sisters in Trujillo," her use of the past tense seemed significant, as if that chapter of her life were over. Sadly, I had observed lately that her memories of Trujillo were becoming hazy. But if, as M. F. Tupper said, memory is the "storehouse of the mind, garner of facts and fancies," then Brenda's memory was highly functional, for when she couldn't remember facts, she substituted fancies without the slightest hesitation. Though on that particular November day, she claimed five siblings, in fact the number fluctuated from week to week—anywhere from one to nineteen—until I became convinced that she herself did not know the exact count. When the birth of septuplets in Iowa became headline news, Brenda, never to be out-done, announced that one day her mother had given birth to ten children—seven boys and three girls. But she didn't want them, so she gave them away to her neighbors in Trujillo. One afternoon, when the girls had an argument about what to watch on TV, Brenda announced that she owned the only television in Trujillo and she could watch whatever she wanted. She didn't have to share her TV because she kept it in her bedroom (as if she had a bedroom). Sometimes when one of my daughters was called away from play for piano practice and no one else was free to play with her, Brenda would loiter near the piano, plinking at the keys and doing whatever she could think of to cause distraction. One day, Grace lost patience with her and told her she was not allowed to touch the piano again. "In Trujillo, we had a piano," she said with pride, "and I could play it any time I wanted. It was better than this old piano," she stated, giving it a derisive kick. "*Our* piano was blue!"

As we passed a school bus one morning, I told Brenda in Spanish that back when I was in school, my mother drove one of those. "I can't believe it!" she cried dramatically in English. Then, in Spanish, she informed me that in Trujillo her mother also drove a school bus. "Not a yellow one, though," she explained. "It was white…" Then after a moment's thought, she said, "No—green."

I looked at my watch and realized we were going to arrive at Brenda's school a bit late that morning and she might miss the gathering time when students lined up outdoors. I prepared her by explaining in both English and Spanish that the other kids might be inside the school building when we got there. As we pulled into the drive, I was surprised to see that the students were still outdoors. "Oh, look!" I said. "They haven't gone in after all."

"Nope," Brenda replied as she climbed out of the van. "They're waiting for me." This reply illustrated the quintessential Brenda— self-confident, expectant, sometimes presumptuous. In a winsome, innocent way, she assumed that the world was there to accommodate her. Rather than making a brat out of her, this perspective gave her the freedom to be generous and, usually, solicitous of everyone around her.

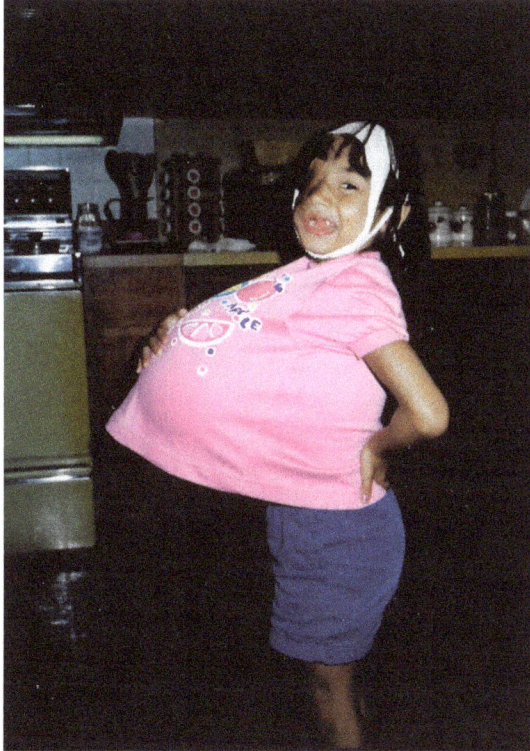

Our playful Brenda, at least two weeks overdue

She took joy in being contrary, usually in a playful way. If I warned her that her soup was hot, she said no, it was cool and took a big bite to prove her point. If I said it was very cold outside and she should wear her long red coat, she said no, the sun was shining and put on her purple spring jacket. She was learning English at an astounding rate and enjoyed wowing us by using big words. One day, she told me in English that when she lived in Trujillo, she and her sister would walk home from school by one of two routes: along the beach or along the road, "whichever was *appropriate*." During dinner, she would report on her school day in English, just like the other children at the table. "The boys were so talkeen, and Mrs. Broderson said, 'Be quiet!' and they were still so talkeen and so runeen." She liked to inform people that she didn't speak Spanish anymore, and it was true: she rarely did. As her Spanish vocabulary slipped away, she would sometimes ask me how to say this or that in Spanish, which she pronounced "Spinach." "How do you say *purple* in Spinach?" "How do you say, 'How old are you?' in Spinach?"

Meanwhile, we saw Dr. Hardy every ten days or so. I could tell from his mutterings that while monitoring Brenda's healing, he was also plotting his next move. He planned a complicated operation in which he would remove a chunk of muscle and skin from Brenda's back, under her shoulder blade, and transplant it to her face, creating a more natural contour and filling the depression left by her crushed skull and the loss of her eye. During the same operation, Dr. Stroncek, an oral surgeon, would work with Dr. Hardy to implant an artificial jaw joint, replacing the defunct one Dr. Hardy had extracted during the summer.

An early morning snowfall on surgery day changed the world from dull gray to fluffy white. Brenda watched the usual morning bustle pensively, waving goodbye as family members left for school and the office. Then she turned from the window, looking a little bereft and very aware that the time had come for our trip across town to the hospital. By eleven o'clock, she was in the operating room, and I was on my way home. Calls from the surgery suite every two hours assured me that things were going well, but as evening approached, I was in a quandary. Rose's school Christmas program was that night, and Brenda was still in surgery: Did I dare go? During the next call from the operating room, I heard Dr. Hardy's voice in the background. "Go to the Christmas program," he advised. "We'll be at this awhile."

Assured that things were going well, we left for Rose's school. The program would take place in the sanctuary of the church next door, and as we waited, I glanced around the room, tastefully decorated with softly lit wreaths and garlanded banisters. Recorded Christmas music played softly in the background. Peace surrounded me, but I was not at peace within. What had happened to the advent season in our home and in my heart? Our advent wreath, usually the focus of our December devotions, had never emerged from storage. We had hardly sung a single carol as a family. I had been so busy nursing Noli through pneumonia and asthma and preparing for Brenda's hospitalization, various parties, and obligatory gift exchanges, that the wonder of Jesus' coming hardly entered my mind. After Bob had taken the girls to a Christmas tree farm earlier in the month, he and I argued about which of us would preside at the decorating: neither of us wanted to. Not only had I let the fun of Christmas traditions slip away; I had failed to emphasize the season's true meaning. I berated myself for failing to set a joyful, expectant mood in our home; for getting caught up in details and obligations; and for sitting at Rose's program wishing I were somewhere else. One by one, classes marched onto the stage. The second graders went up, and there was our darling Rose in her blue flowered dress, singing and gesturing with gusto. Even as I gazed at my own daughter, my thoughts were with Brenda and Dr. Hardy, now about ten hours into the operation.

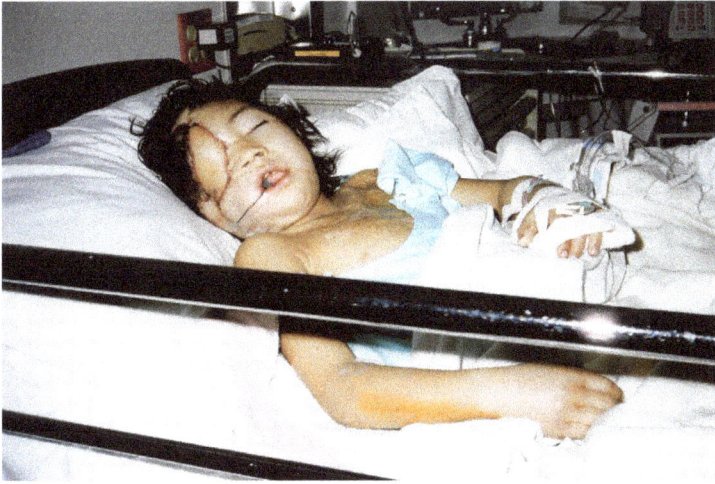

Brenda after twelve hours in the operating room

We returned home, congratulated Rose, gave the kids a snack, and tucked them into bed, all the time waiting for the phone to ring. Shortly after ten o'clock, the call came. One more hour and Brenda's surgery would be over. I drove to the hospital. A little before 1 a.m., Brenda arrived on the pediatric floor. Doctors and nurses carefully monitored the surgeons' handiwork, checking frequently for a strong pulse, which indicated a good blood supply to the graft. Slightly feverish, swollen, and unable to speak around a plastic wedge placed between her teeth, Brenda croaked unintelligible complaints between bouts of nausea. There was nothing practical I could do to relieve her misery. She seemed very small in her adult-sized hospital bed. The graft looked to me like a piece of crazy quilt stitched to her face, and I felt a deep melancholy that was not lessened by the songs of Christmas joy I had heard from children's voices just a few hours before. The situation seemed hopeless, the surgery pointless. Brenda was a torn-up, broken child. Why were we kidding ourselves? No matter how skilled her surgeons, no matter how much pain we put her through, no matter how many operations she endured, Brenda would never look normal.

After she fell into a deep, morphine-induced sleep, I drove home, where the dog greeted me with a gruffly quiet welcoming bark. I went from room to room, lingering over the beds of my children, their comely faces half-buried in their pillows. Reaching down to touch Brenda's empty pillow, I said a silent prayer for her comfort. I slipped into my nightgown and crawled into bed beside Bob, but sleep would not come. I forced my thoughts away from Brenda and onto the true meaning of Christmas—the incarnation of Jesus. "Surely he took up our infirmities and carried our sorrows"—even the infirmities of a small impaired boy and the sorrows of a little disfigured girl. The meaning of Jesus' birth came to me quietly, in the context of my very real world, my burdens, and the day I had just lived through. Half-asleep, Bob wrapped his arms around me. Even enfolded in the arms of my soul mate, I felt alone but not unpleasantly so. For a long time, I lay in the silent, peaceful darkness, thinking about truth revealed in spite of—or even by way of—our day-to-day reality and cares, the sorrows He came to help us carry.

Being hospitalized at Christmastime has its compensations.

After eight days in the hospital, Brenda was discharged just in time for her first American Christmas. As I packed for our trip to visit family in Michigan, she flitted about the house, seeming to be everywhere at once, a busy little body needing to release the excitement, energy, and anticipation that had been pent up during her confinement. She told us all, several times each day, that she loved us. She declared Bob her favorite daddy. (Out of how many? I wondered.) When Kate gave her a locket containing a picture of herself, Brenda showed it to me with delight. "I love my necklace," she said, "because now I can look at Kate all the time."

Our gift exchange with Bob's family in Michigan proved once again that his siblings—two single professionals, indulgent to a fault—would have tried to procure the moon if one of their nieces wanted it. Our daughters knew from experience that giving Aunt Joan and Uncle Paul their Christmas wish list was as good as placing an order. But Brenda was overwhelmed with joy as her every desire came true, wrapped in shiny paper and ribbon and placed beneath the beautifully adorned tree.

We returned home with a week of vacation to go and a plethora of new Barbie accessories to fill it. The basement soon became Barbieville, complete with houses and stores—even a cash register which ran credit checks on Barbie's Visa card and said, "Credit approved. Thank you. Have a nice day!" One day, as I walked through the basement to the laundry room, I had the eerie sense of passing through a war zone; about seventy naked Barbie dolls of all ages and both genders were heaped on the table like so many corpses. I was informed that the Barbies were being divided up into families. How nice, except for several old, shorn, maimed, or dismembered Barbies who were tossed off to the side. For these hapless dolls, there would be no families, no Christmas, no malls, and no credit cards.

We did not know then that Christmas week was the calm before the storm. Shortly after New Year's Day, Dr. Stroncek ordered therapy to stretch a tight band of accumulated scar tissue in Brenda's jaw and to keep the new artificial joint flexible and functional. This painful procedure had to be done at home three times a day, in thirty-minute torture sessions. I hated them as much as Brenda did. Remarkably, she jumped off the rack after each session without a backward glance, chewing a hunk of bubblegum, which she received not only as a reward but as part of her therapy. Whenever she was not chewing gum, eating, or having therapy, Brenda had to wear a plastic wedge, called a bite block, between her teeth. Dr. Stroncek's goal was to enable her to open her mouth, chew, and eat normally. As time passed, we saw progress, which she would proudly point out during meals: "Look, Mom, I'm using my spoon! My hands are clean!" When I recalled the way she had been eating when she came to our home—cramming little bits of food between her clenched teeth as crumbs and chunks fell to the floor—I realized that the gains she was making were worth the pain and tears.

When Christmas vacation ended, Brenda was anxious to return to her social life at school. Her English teachers and Mrs. Broderson marveled at the language skills and vocabulary she had acquired in her month away from the classroom. Then, all of a sudden that January, phonics clicked for her. Up to that point, the spelling tests she brought home had all looked the same: sheets of large-lined paper with a column of numbers scrawled down the left side. Where the spelling words should have appeared, there were only scribbles, loops, and zigzags. But now that she got it, she took up spelling with gusto. If a school bus passed us on the road, up went her forefinger, as she shouted with a big smile, "B-u-s!" If a jogger crossed at the light: "R-u-n!" In the hospital elevator: "U-p!" As Bob observed, "There's no stopping her now. She's bound for the head of the class."

Meanwhile, Rose was facing her own academic challenges. On the first day back to school, she brought home a parent letter announcing that the class was about to study borrowing in math: would all parents please make sure their children were well-rested, thoroughly breakfasted, and alert during the remainder of the week? When Rose appeared at our bedside that night, crying and complaining of stomach pain, I first thought it was a case of nerves, as she had spent a good part of the evening fretting about borrowing. What the teacher had said to inspire such angst I could only imagine. But, alas, Rose was worse in the morning and spent the day in bed with a bowl beside her pillow. Between bouts of nausea and intermittent naps, she stewed about missing math on such an important day: "When am I going to learn borrowing?" she fretted.

The next day, Brenda brought home notices that her class had been exposed to strep throat and chicken pox. Thankfully, she dodged both of those bullets. But she could not dodge the daily pain of therapy. During a recheck appointment, Dr. Stroncek ordered that her bite block be worn on the injured side of her mouth at least half the time. (Up to this point, it had been inserted between her teeth on the undamaged and much less sensitive side of her jaw.) Following this pronouncement, he asked Brenda to open her mouth as far as she could and quickly packed it in almost before she knew what had happened. Her piercing cries of pain sent him running for a narcotic painkiller. That took the edge off, but she glowered at me all the way home. Our house was a sad place that weekend, as we all sympathized with the pain-weary Brenda. She ate little and complained of stomachaches. Often I found her sitting in corners with her head in her hands. Whenever I had to insert the bite block on the injured side of her mouth, she would reflexively fight me. The only way I could stop her writhing and keep her still enough for the procedure was to lay her out on the floor and sit on top of her. After the dastardly deed was done, the initial pain would be intolerable. Her screams and cries exerted so much pressure on the top of her head that blood seeped through the bandages from her open scalp wound, which had not bled for months. The girls would gather round with tears in their eyes until one of them was called upon to comfort Noli, who invariably cried in sympathy or fear, even though we had tucked him away in a distant bedroom.

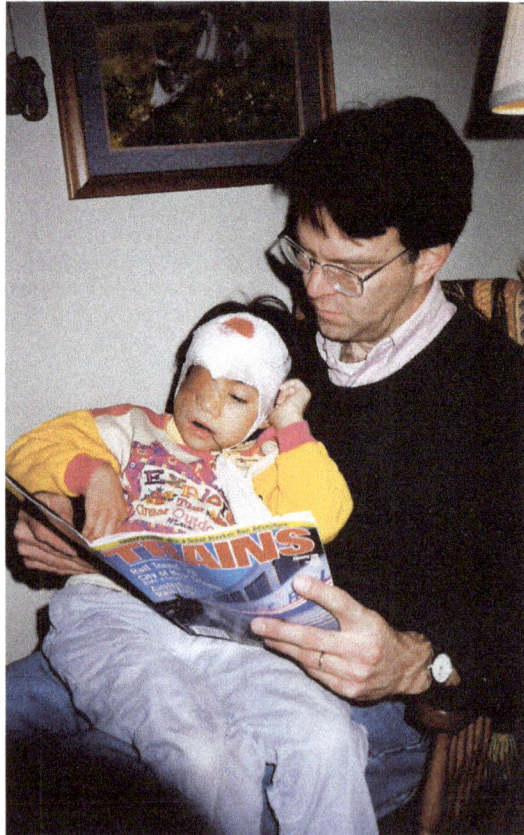

Brenda finds comfort on Bob's lap after a home therapy session.

I appealed to the tenderhearted Dr. Hardy. I was sure he didn't want to collude in Brenda's suffering any more than I did, and I was hoping in the worst way that he would tell me I didn't have to hurt her anymore. But he sadly admitted that her jaw therapy was not within his purview. Then, about the time I thought I couldn't subject her to even one more torture session, the pain decreased, as the scar tissue on the injured side of her mouth yielded enough to accommodate the bite block. Getting it in was still a struggle, but after a few minutes, she would come to me with a look of pleasant surprise. "It doesn't hurt so much anymore," she might say, shrugging happily. During her twice-weekly occupational therapy sessions at the hospital, her therapists monitored her mobility by asking her to open her mouth as far as possible while they measured the distance between her top and bottom teeth. It was gratifying to see therapy bringing about the desired change; but every fraction of a millimeter was won through multiple sessions of blood, sweat, and tears. I mean this literally, as she cried, broke out in sweats and often bled from her gums, loosened teeth, or scalp wound. I knew her therapy sessions would be indelibly fixed in my memory in all their sad detail. Her cries and moans, her furrowed brow, her busy hands—one clutching a washcloth to her chin and the other hanging onto my shirt or patting my cheek beseechingly. Her words repeated so often: "Be gentle, be gentle, go slow, no more, no more!" Even as she pleaded with me, however, she endeavored to cooperate. If I delayed a therapy session, she would remind me. If I miscounted repetitions, she would correct me, usually through tears. Our sympathy for each other was like a circle: I pitied her for the pain I had to inflict, and she had compassion on me because she knew that hurting her also caused me pain.

One night, when I folded back the blankets on my bed, I found a note left on my pillow. Though the handwriting was Kate's, the signature was Brenda's, and the grammatical error confirmed that Kate had written it exactly as dictated: "Dear mom, I love you very much. You are my favorite mom. Thank you to do therapy with me, mom. Love, Brenda."

Chapter 4

B y early February, Brenda and I had been to forty-four medical appointments together since her arrival in June. During that winter of therapy, our daily battle with scar tissue and pain felt like an inexorable consignment—not only during each session but beforehand because we knew it was coming and afterward while we recovered. I turned into a lean, mean therapy machine. Instead of pressing weights, I pressed scar tissue, and my chicken muscles developed into respectable biceps. I also came to realize that the result of all this effort would not be constant, steady improvement. Brenda and I would no sooner celebrate a victory than the contracting forces of adhesions and scar tissue would take back the hill we had just won through so much hard work and suffering.

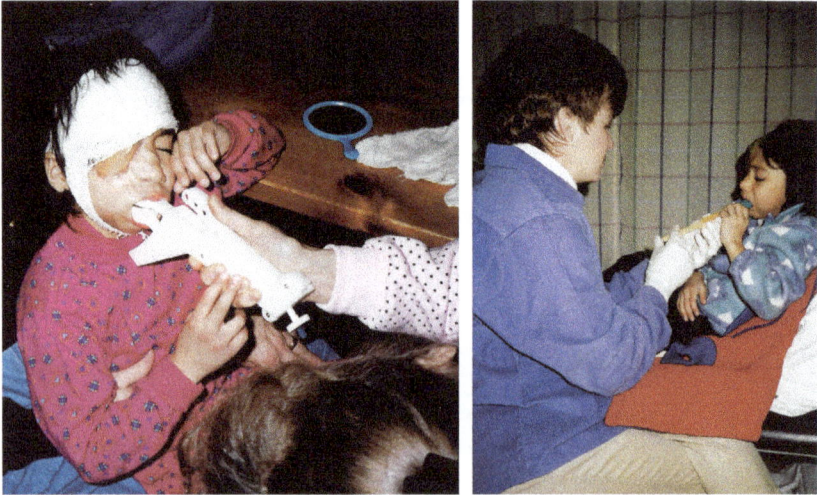

Painful therapy sessions at the hospital (right, with
Brenda's favorite therapist, Gaye) and (left) at home

With the natural resilience of children, my own kids adapted to our routine as if it were normal to inflict extreme pain on a six-year-old child three times a day. They had friends in, carried on conversations, and reviewed spelling words over the tortured screams of my little victim. I didn't know whether their comment to a visitor—that they hardly noticed Brenda's therapy anymore—should comfort me or worry me. Which was worse: the tearful sympathy they felt at first or their acquired indifference to what was going on right in the same room?

Concerned that I seemed down during phone conversations, my mom offered to fly out for a visit. Our two weeks of leisurely outings, laughter, conversation, and practical help with meals and childcare were like a restorative; and her presence brought a welcome cheer to our home. As she shared a story from her youth during dinner one night, the girls wanted to know how old she was when the incident happened. "I'm not sure," Mom answered, "but I guess I was somewhere between sixteen and eighteen."

Rose looked puzzled. "Grandma," she said, "wouldn't that be seventeen?" She may have missed those classes on borrowing, but Rose could still do math.

As her visit neared its end, Mom and I commented repeatedly on the wonderful time we'd both had. However, as if she needed to pay homage to the intense suffering she had witnessed, Mom always qualified her statement: "…except for Brenda's therapy." She often commented—sometimes with tears—on the complexity of Brenda's care and the medical maze we were winding our way through.

"Well, we started out with a straightforward heart case," I said, referring to our twelve-year-old foster child Eyra, whose one cardiac operation had remedied her life-threatening problem. "I guess we could look at this as a promotion. You might say we're climbing the corporate ladder."

"In that case, I hope you won't have to go too much higher," Mom answered with a sigh.

After my mother left, the burden of managing our kids' daily life fell squarely on my shoulders again, and if Mama ain't organized,

45

ain't nobody organized. Like most other busy parents, I found the early morning hours the most hectic, and I did whatever I could each evening to prepare for the next day: making sandwiches, pureeing foods for Noli's lunch, washing eyeglasses, signing permission slips, collecting school books, snow pants, mittens, shoes, and all the other paraphernalia my kids would cram into their backpacks in the morning. Each evening, the girls laid out clothing and hair accessories while I sorted laundry for the next day's washing.

Starting at 5 a.m. each school day, I had three carefully choreographed hours to get my family out the door and to their respective locations. I packed lunches, woke Noli, gave him his morning doses of medicine, fed him, brushed his hair, changed his diaper, put on his splints, dressed him, and put him on the floor to play. Because Brenda's persistent weeping scalp wounds had to be covered at school, she wore bandages; her school days began with early morning baths to soak the previous day's wraps off. As she did this, I would put a towel in the oven to warm for her and run downstairs to throw in the first load of laundry. At 6:30 a.m., I began waking the remaining children by snapping up window shades; singing irritating ditties; and instructing the dog to bark and jump on their beds, which she did with great relish. While my daughters dragged themselves from their warm blankets, I bandaged Brenda's head and got her settled at the breakfast table with a bowl of hot cereal or "Rice Christmas Trees"—the name she had given Rice Krispies over the holidays. About this time, Bob would return from his three-mile morning walk and join her. Even on the coldest mornings, he smelled like he had just worked out at the gym, and this was the cause of much nose holding and drama on Brenda's part. Bob would respond by sidling up beside her, singing, "They call me Mr. Sweat Ball…"

At 7 a.m., I made sure Laura was seated in front of the morning news—her daily current events assignment. At 7:01, I endeavored to get the other four girls away from the television and back on task. One by one, they would find something palatable and carry their breakfast to the table where a little eating was accompanied by a lot of jostling, squabbling, nudging, tattling, and staring each other down. About this time, Brenda would start to complain of a nervous stomachache as the time for her therapy approached. While she and I kept our appointment with pain, I would ask the nearest idle child to get Noli bundled up and into his wheelchair, ready for his bus. While keeping one eye on the driveway and one hand in Brenda's mouth, I urged everyone to brush their teeth, put on boots and coats, gather their things, and stop arguing about whose turn it was to sit in the front seat. Then I would recruit whichever daughter seemed the most ready, settle Brenda in her lap, and insert her bite block as Brenda yelled, cried, and begged me to be gentle.

By 7:30, I was standing at the front door, keys in hand, yelling departure information. After one last check for left-behind lunches, mittens, and books, we piled out the door into the van. We picked up the other three children in our carpool, then started the morning "bus run," as I dropped children off at three different schools. After all this dropping off, I would gratefully drop into a chair at home, closing my eyes to dirty dishes on the counter, a wet towel on the floor, and the barrettes I forgot to put in Rose's hair.

You'd think that on weekends, we would all be grateful to stay home. But kids are just as energetic on Saturday and Sunday as on any other day, if not more so. Our two foster children could not engage in cold-weather fun such as sledding and ice-skating: Noli because of his impairments and Brenda because doctors' orders prohibited any activity that might result in a blow to the face or head. With six children ages six to fourteen, family outings were essential to keep us from going stir crazy during the cold months of winter. Our budget didn't allow for expensive museums, movies, or weekends at indoor water parks. So Activities Director Sylvia Boomsma was ever alert for outings which were free and open to the public. We discovered that the state capitol was open on weekends and was, aside from a few security guards, almost deserted. Its cavernous hallways offered space for children to run, holler, and enjoy the echoes of their own voices. It was like being in a cave but without the inconveniences of utter darkness, treacherously wet paths, and unseen drop-offs. One Sunday afternoon in February, while Bob and the kids ran happily down a capitol hallway, ducking behind pillars and corners to hide from each other, I ducked into a women's restroom and headed for a stall. As I sat there taking care of business, I heard five girls straggle in one at a time, each asking the same question: "Where's Mom?" Our family almost monopolized the facilities; however, one woman who had preceded me into the restroom emerged from her stall after I did.

"Good grief!" she exclaimed. "You must have about ten kids. All I keep hearing is, 'Where's Mom?' 'Where's Mom?' 'Where's Mom?'" We laughed as she washed up and left the room.

One by one, my own did the same until I found myself waiting for one last straggler. After quite a time had passed, I called out, "What is this? Your big poop of the day?" At last, the dawdler emerged—a professional woman, smartly dressed in a stylish suit. "Oh!" I laughed. "You're not one of my kids, are you?"

"No, I'm not," she replied. Her very serious tone and austere expression told me that she was mighty glad of it too.

Noli had a seemingly firm prospect for adoption that winter. A single woman from Milwaukee had expressed strong interest. The possibility that he would leave saddened us because we loved Noli. But it also gladdened us because we knew that for several reasons, we were not the right permanent family for him. When he arrived from the Philippines, we had agreed to provide foster care for three months, and he had been with us for almost two years. So the sooner he found his long-term placement, the better. Despite several phone conversations between his would-be mother and myself, I sensed that she didn't fully grasp the limits of Noli's intellect and abilities. She had arranged piano lessons, shopped computers, and even selected a dog for him. On the day of her scheduled visit to our home, we conspired to present Noli at his best, brightest, and most appealing. We made sure he was well rested, well-fed, well washed, and dressed in his most flattering ensemble. The visit started out well, but I could see the woman's interest waning as she looked around our living room at Noli's change table, Noli's wheelchair, Noli's stander, and the toys we had suspended from ceiling hooks for him to bat at while rolling about. During her visit, he resorted to some of his less attractive behaviors—cocking his right fist and whacking himself repeatedly in the head, knocking kitchen stools into walls, and slamming cupboard doors. I could see that all our preparations, and Noli's beguiling smiles and giggles, had been for naught. We later learned that our visitor hurried home and immediately called the adoption agency to tell Noli's caseworker that under no circumstances could she parent Noli for the rest of her life. And in my heart of hearts, I knew she was right. This was not the first time this had happened, and though we were disappointed, we had long ago accepted the uncertainty of Noli's future. We would continue to enjoy his sweet nature for as long as he was with us.

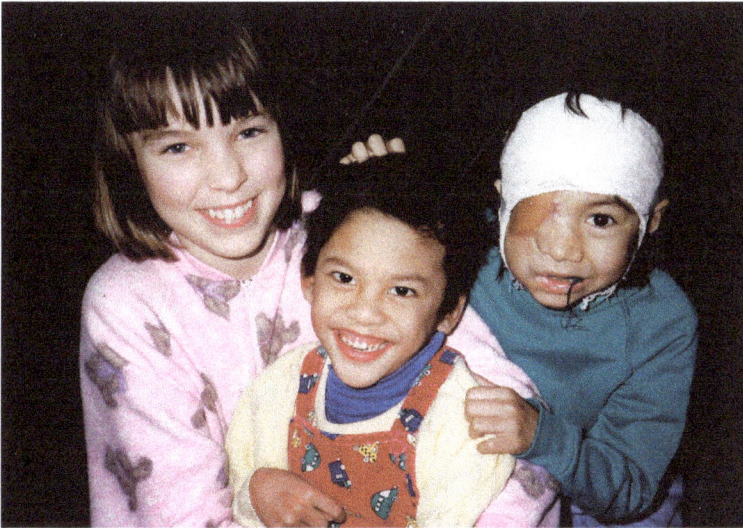

Okay, sure... We'll keep Noli a little longer.

Winter wore on; and our three-bedroom ranch home, always a beehive of activity, seemed to grow smaller and more crowded. Nights rarely passed without interruption. A mother's sense of something amiss would awaken me from a deep sleep. Beside my bed, a pale face would be peering silently at me through the darkness. Brenda needed pain medication, or Noli was crying, or Kate was sleepwalking, or someone had a nightmare and needed comforting.

Kate, Rose, and Brenda, who shared their bedroom with Noli, had sleeping bags stashed behind the couch and would move to the living room to doze through Noli's crying spells, which could last an hour or more. (He didn't seem distraught—just at loose ends because he couldn't sleep.)

The "teen bedroom" was Grace's and Laura's. We wanted them to have a space they could call their own, where they could entertain their friends, decorate as they wished, and have a sense of grownup independence. The two roommates were very different people. The quiet, introverted Laura cared little about what was trending and rarely had guests. She spent much of her time at her workbench in the basement, cranking out one clever creation after another, made mostly from plastic doodads or scraps of wood she found about the house or at school. The more social Grace sometimes got caught up in the latest teen craze, and this made for frequent redecorating. That winter, Dalmatians—the past year's fixation—suddenly became "dumb." Posters came down; figurines were hidden away at the back of the closet; and the dotted, spotted half of the teen room became a blank slate ready for the next adornment. The new fixation was the movie *Titanic,* which had recently taken youthful America by storm. After Grace and a friend saw the three-hour-and-thirty-minute saga in the theater, she pestered the rest of us endlessly to join her for her second viewing. Titanic posters plastered the walls on her side of the bedroom. Trivia related to the film—and sometimes even the historical event—peppered our conversation for weeks. Grace thought that the love affair of Jack and Rose, the movie's main characters, was the most tragic story ever told. Just for the sake of argument, I asked whether she didn't find other Titanic vignettes even more tragic; for example, what about fathers who put their wives and children on lifeboats and said goodbye, knowing that it was forever? After all, Jack and Rose were little more than acquaintances, having known each other only a few days in what some might call a tawdry love affair. I politely declined invitations to join Grace for a trip to the theater. "I already see a sad movie three times a day," I remarked, "every time Brenda has therapy."

Perhaps I've given the impression that Bob wasn't very involved in our family's foster care project. In some ways, he wasn't. He certainly assented to it, and since it was happening in his own home, he could hardly be disinterested. But international medical foster care was my hobby. His was building a model railroad in the basement, an interest for which he had precious little time, thanks in part to this family commitment of ours. I didn't expect Bob's hands-on involvement in my hobby, any more than I wanted to be deeply involved in his. We had an unspoken agreement that I would take our foster children to appointments, do their therapy, change their diapers, and sit at their bedsides in the hospital. But it wasn't as if he ignored them. Though he spoke barely a word of Spanish, he reached out to every foster child with playful teasing, good cheer, and affection. He was the parent whose arms were always open to little ones who needed comfort, the daddy who gave them piggyback rides down the hallway at bedtime. He was our teenage foster children's errand boy; they knew that they need only look at him longingly and say, *"Hamburguesa,"* and he would make a late-night run to McDonald's. He was the generous papa who took our foster kids shopping to buy gifts for the vast array of relatives back home. Eyra, age twelve, and Arlette, age sixteen, were our first two foster children, in Madison concurrently for cardiac operations. Arlette had been given money by her family to buy toiletry items and other small gifts. Eyra had no money but was only too willing to spend Arlette's or ours. One evening, when the girls wanted to go shopping, they made puppy-dog eyes at Bob; and soon the three of them were off to a local discount superstore. Somehow, Arlette conveyed that she needed to buy underwear for her father, so Bob led the girls to the men's department. Now they were faced with selecting the correct size and type. Using improvised sign language, Bob tried to ask Arlette what size her dad wore and whether he would want briefs or boxers. Seeing a few loose pairs of undershorts lying on a shelf, he began holding them up to his own waist, trying with exaggerated motions to ask if her dad was bigger or smaller than this. About this time, a large woman in a Green Bay Packers sweatshirt walked slowly past, observing Bob's gesticulations and his two young companions. She glared at Bob, and her expression said it all: *What is this? Some kind of perverse charades game?* Bob shrugged, embarrassed and as tongue-tied for English as he had been for Spanish just a moment earlier. "Hmph," the woman said, and shuffled off.

One of the reasons Bob and I had little trouble parsing out roles in an agreeable way was that we both came from a very traditional background. Underwear were white. Doctors were men; nurses were women. Wives cleaned, cooked, washed clothes, and cared for children. Husbands worked in offices, took care of the family car, did home repairs, mowed the lawn, and shoveled snow. Though such a view was hardly the norm in progressive Madison, it made for a neatly delineated marriage and peace in our home. It gave me the freedom to be a full-time mother to our children and foster children. However, it also meant that Bob might come home to a harried wife who hadn't managed to make dinner, or no wife at all, because she was at the hospital with one of our foster kids. Bob rarely returned to a peaceful house, a well-rested mate, or a quiet place to put up his feet and read the paper after a stressful day at the office. This was especially true after he and I exchanged the master bedroom—now full of kids—for the smallest bedroom in the house, directly across from the doorway to the kitchen. A double bed and a small dresser left just enough room to navigate around the furniture. The closet was so small that Bob kept his clothes, shoes, and other personal belongings in the basement, near "the boys' bathroom." Good natured as usual, he came up with several affectionate names for our room, including "the servants' quarters" and "the walk-in closet." Bob often joked about our estrogen-enriched environment and referred to himself by irreverent nicknames like "the only rooster at the hen party" or "nursemaid to a bunch of women." But there was never any doubt that Bob—a big man with a big voice and a big personality—was clearly and incontestably the head of this motley outfit.

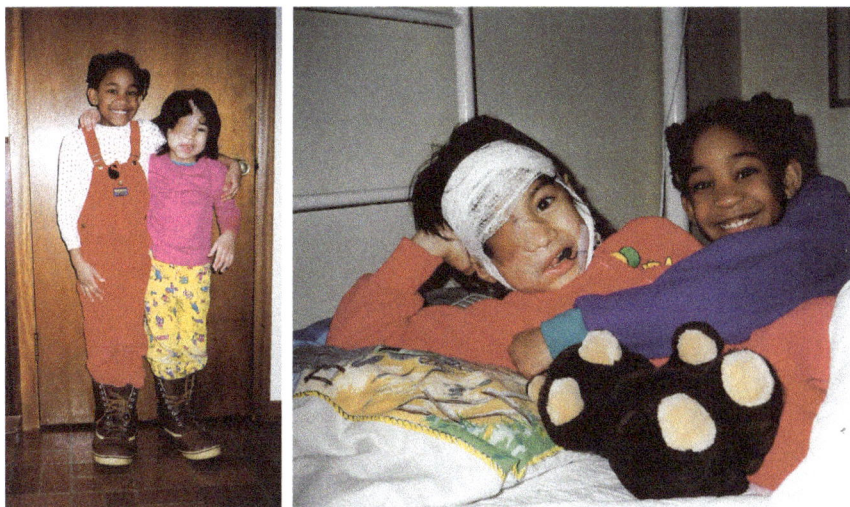

Rose and Brenda—bedfellows and fast friends

Chapter 5

In April, after four months of therapy, Brenda's oral surgeon ordered a hiatus. It came just in time. Brenda and I were both discouraged because progress had stalled and her pain seemed pointless. If only therapy were ending because we had reached our goal, how wonderful life would be. But in fact, the doctor had ordered this stay because we had achieved all we could through therapy—and precious little it was.

Dr. Stroncek began to talk about more jaw surgery, but who wanted to think about that? For Brenda and me, suddenly released from the daily routine that caused us both so much pain, life was fun again. The dark cloud that had hung over us every hour of the past four months was lifted! As the pale sunshine and chill breezes of early spring began melting away the vestiges of a dark, cold winter, Brenda seemed suffused with new life. She mastered the elements of reading and began to read simple books from cover to cover. When she had homework assignments, she happily seated herself at the kitchen table to "study" with her sisters. I became aware of her astounding ability to memorize as I watched her prepare for spelling tests. Each Monday, after a quick review of her newly assigned word list, she would quiz herself, writing the entire list of ten words in order without looking. She could even remember the spelling of words which had no meaning to her because she had never learned them. I realized this when she asked for pronunciations: "How do you say the word c-r-e-e-p-i-n-g?"

Meanwhile, she was acquiring English by leaps and bounds. Near the end of the school year, her ESL teachers stopped teaching her English and started reviewing Spanish with her, anticipating that she might return to Honduras during the summer. One day, she climbed into the van after school and proudly announced that she could say *water* in Spanish: "*Agua!*" She had mentally filed her

Spanish in some deep recess and often asked me how to say the simplest words—*dog, house, egg*—in Spanish.

For the first time since she'd started school in the fall, Brenda didn't have to miss a couple of half days each week to visit the surgery clinic or her occupational therapists. She was living an almost normal life. She was excited about the spring music program at her school and prepared diligently. The theme was "Songs of the Sixties," and each afternoon, she would spread out several pages of lyrics from golden oldies like "Scarborough Fair," "Yellow Submarine," and "Feelin' Groovy." Announcing that she had to practice, she would begin to sing in her tuneless way, "If I had a hamburger, I'd hamber in the mornin'."

All of our foster children from other countries were tone-deaf when they arrived and seemed completely unaware of it. I never knew the reason for this, except that they may not have learned to sing in music classes or Sunday school, as our kids did. Or perhaps American music was just that different. But they all took to music with enthusiasm. When it was their turn to choose a recording for the ride to school, they mulled over our array of cassette tapes like kids in a candy store. When we sang prayers at the supper table, they joined in with gusto, never holding back.

One spring day, while we traveled across town to the clinic, Brenda bounced in the front seat, singing along to the soundtrack of Disney's *Pocahontas*. As the cassette tape clicked to the end of the current side, she said sadly, "They didn't play my favorite song, 'Just Around the Rubber Band'" ("Just Around the River Bend").

"Oh, don't worry," I said in a reassuring voice. "The tape will turn over in a minute, and then you'll hear your favorite song."

She studied the narrow slot with a furrowed brow, wondering how a cassette could turn over in such a small space. She looked at me skeptically, perhaps wondering if I were teasing her. Within moments, the tape reversed, and the other side began to play. She settled back in her seat and patted the armrest affectionately. "This van is so *cute*," she declared.

Brenda's furlough ended in late April when Dr. Hardy operated again, placing a large tissue expander under her scalp. This expander's external port—a white plastic tube sticking out through the crown of

Brenda's head—was a bit unsightly; but it allowed us to inject fluid at home and saved us one or two trips to the clinic each week. Dr. Hardy examined her scalp every ten days or so and, if all seemed well, gave her a generous injection in the clinic. Because he was starting to feel pressed for time as we approached the one-year mark, he put Brenda's skin expansion on the fast track.

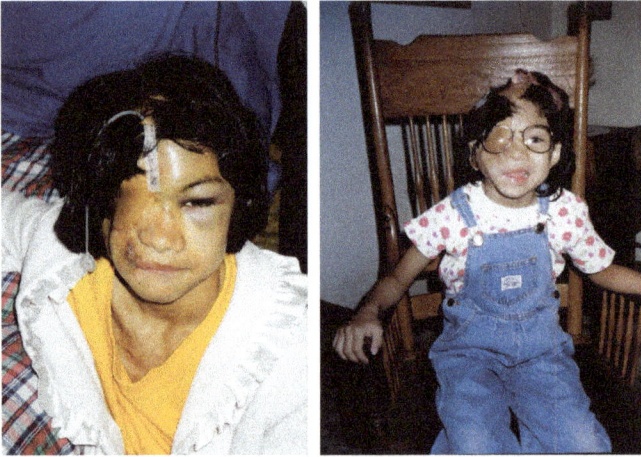

Infections, extrusions, and setbacks were frequent occurences in Brenda's medical odyssey.

Man's best friend can help us through the rough patches. Henna, our Dutch Shepherd, was Brenda's constant companion, comforter, protector, and playmate.

By early June, Brenda's head was once again lumpy, bumpy, heavy, and sore. One night, a few days after a large injection, she came to my bedside complaining that her head hurt and her pillow was wet. I turned on the light and was surprised to see that her expander had extruded in two places and half of it was hanging out of a large hole in her scalp.

"Brenda, what happened!?" Dr. Hardy cried as he came into the examining room the next day. He had seen her only days before, and all seemed well then. He didn't know why her skin had deteriorated so quickly; a pocket of infection was the most likely culprit. Dr. Hardy was obviously disappointed and almost incredulous. "This is the most impressively abrupt extrusion I've ever seen," he told his passel of white-coated students. "That thing's gotta come out."

When he asked how long ago Brenda had eaten, I realized he wanted to take her to the operating room that very afternoon. We'd had lunch just before leaving for the appointment, so that ruled out immediate surgery. It was Friday afternoon, and time was running out. It was unlikely that surgery would be scheduled for the weekend, except in a life-threatening emergency.

"Are you sure you can't drain it and take it out right here while she's awake?" I asked.

Dr. Hardy looked at Brenda dubiously. Of course it was an option, he replied, but it might be difficult and painful, and Brenda was only seven. "Just try," I urged, and as he called for a nurse and supplies, I primed Brenda. Turning my back to the circle of ubiquitous students, I took her on my lap and spoke to her in a soothing voice, as if we were the only two people in the room.

"If you can be very brave right now," I said, "it's possible you won't have to come back for surgery." She nodded trustingly. Though she wasn't sure what she was in for, she would try to cooperate.

As Dr. Hardy drained the expander and snipped the tube, Brenda seemed nervous and jumpy. "Now I'm just going to wipe your head," he said gently, approaching with a gauze pad in his gloved hand. *Slooop...* He skillfully eased the expander out before Brenda realized what had happened. Surprised by the sharp, momentary pain, she shed a few tears. But her distress was soon forgotten as we all praised her for her bravery. Dr. Hardy hugged her. The nurses gave her stickers, hugs, and congratulations. Even the white-coated students came to life, patting her on the back and high-fiving her. When she asked to see the errant expander, Dr. Hardy fished it out of the trash, rinsed it off, and gave it to her as a souvenir. "Is there anything else I can do for you?" he asked.

"Ask him for the moon," I told Brenda jokingly. But in fact, I felt as though Dr. Hardy had already given us the moon, because I was so relieved that we had evaded yet one more trip to the operating room.

Medical crises were the order of the day at our house. Compared to asthma, extrusions, infections, complications, and elective and emergency operations on our foster children, my own children's more mundane complaints seemed minor, even insignificant. Bumps, scrapes, rashes, and sore throats got little reaction from me. Most such ailments would resolve on their own, and I was no more eager than the kids were for more visits to the doctor. One hot summer day, when Brenda had a recheck appointment with Dr. Hardy, Kate went along for the ride. As usual, things were behind schedule in the surgery clinic, and after we had waited more than an hour in a small cubicle, the girls needed to release their pent-up energy. They began playing on a rolling swivel stool—standard issue in every examination room—and were soon spinning each other hard and fast. All of a sudden, centrifugal force overpowered the hapless Kate, sending her backward off the stool and against a sharp corner. Staggering dramatically, she threw herself on the examining table and feigned death, crossing her hands on her chest. As she rose from the dead a moment later, I glanced up from my magazine and noticed blood dripping onto the paper sheet and down the back of Kate's white shirt onto the floor. "Good timing, Kate," I commented, parting her hair for a better look. "If you had to do it, you picked the right place." Grabbing some gauze squares and applying pressure to her wound, I directed the girls' attention to a quieter game—tic-tac-toe on the examining-room whiteboard.

At last, Dr. Hardy appeared with an entourage of students trailing behind him. Brenda wasted no time reporting Kate's accident. "Let me see that, Kate," he said, parting her hair as I had done. "You've got a good little scalp laceration there," he commented. "I'd definitely get a few stitches in that." However, not being Kate's doctor—and being way behind schedule—he did not offer to do the job himself.

Kate and I conferred on the way home. "Feels *fine*," she said pointedly, "just fine. Remember, I'm known as a quick healer." It didn't take much to dissuade me from turning down the street that led to our pediatrician's office. To Kate's relief, we continued toward home and dinner.

Bob received the news as soon as he arrived home from work and took a careful look at the seeping wound. "Bean," he said in a mildly irritated tone, "that's a pretty deep cut. I think Dr. Hardy was right."

I could hardly argue that point. "Of course he was right," I said in a defensive voice. "He went to school for about twenty-seven years. Our daughter's half-inch gash was assessed by a craniofacial reconstruction specialist in what has to be one of the most absurd cases of overqualification in medical history."

"So why didn't you get it sewed up?" Bob's paucity of words was eloquent. Fearing I had erred, I checked on Kate's scalp regularly until bedtime. When I found not a drop of blood on her pillow the next morning, I felt somewhat vindicated. Perhaps I had based my decision upon good judgment and not just the inconvenience of yet another doctor visit. Perhaps...

On Monday, June 22, Noli left us for an adoptive placement that came seemingly out of nowhere. Barbara, his prospective adoptive mother, cared for special needs children not as a hobby but as a career. She had adopted about a dozen kids with disabilities and impairments. Hired staff helped her care for them. In effect, she was running a small institution in her Connecticut home, funded by monthly adoption subsidies and other assistance which some of her children received. While sitting up with a sick child one night, she discovered Noli on an Internet adoption site. Barbara knew immediately that Noli would fit well in her family. The next day, she made the necessary contacts and set the process in motion. Just a couple of weeks later, she traveled to Madison to spend a weekend in our home, observing Noli and talking with us. I took this to be the first step in a long process. But on Monday, Barbara left as suddenly as she had appeared, taking Noli with her. It was almost as if a large bird had swooped down upon our home and carried Noli away on her wings.

I wandered around the house at loose ends. Though I was glad Noli had found a home, it was not what I'd hoped for. I wanted him to be the beloved special child in a "normal"—and preferably large, boisterous, happy—family. Yet I knew that such a placement would not mean nearly as much to Noli as it did to me. Noli would be Noli no matter where he was. As long as his physical needs were met and his world included a few balls and cupboard doors, he'd be the same contented little fellow he had been while he lived with us.

Barbara called after one week to let us know that Noli was indeed the same contented little fellow. His transition to his new home was easy for everyone, and her other children welcomed him with open arms. "It's like he's always been here," Barbara exclaimed happily. For our family, the transition to life without Noli was almost as painless. The girls saw him off that Monday morning with smiles and hugs but no tears. Though his departure left an empty space and they missed him, we all began to enjoy a forgotten freedom, often remarking that outings were sure a lot easier without Noli. It was like a chapter of our life had ended in a good way and at the right time. In fact, the Noli chapter had given us all a greater sense of compassion and patience for the Nolis of this world. We felt a sense of satisfaction with a job well done, a family project completed. Unperturbed, we commended Noli to Barbara's care and contentedly pictured him in his new home, complete with a new ball suspended from the ceiling, which Barbara had installed before even coming to Wisconsin.

A few days after Noli's departure, Brenda faced surgery again— her fifth in a year. The doctors predicted a four-hour operation. She and I looked knowingly at each other and said, "Okay, so six hours." Brenda's operations were never routine; the contents of her head had been so rearranged that each procedure was like exploring uncharted territory. As Dr. Stroncek said, "Every time we go in there, we find some unpleasant surprise. In fact," he continued ominously, "this will probably be the most difficult operation I've done in five years or more."

The challenge facing Dr. Stroncek was to remove the artificial jaw joint he had installed in December. Because Brenda's body considered that joint a foreign object and refused to make peace with it, the troubles that began late in the course of her therapy only worsened until the new joint had become almost immobilized. Now the two surgeons planned to build a new jaw fashioned from the cartilage in Brenda's own rib—a material we all hoped would be peaceably assimilated by the surrounding tissue and would remain elastic over time.

The two surgeons emerged from the operating room after about six hours, feeling pleased and optimistic. They were able to do all they had hoped, and more. When they were finished fashioning a new mandible joint from Brenda's rib, Dr. Hardy looked at the remaining bone and had an inspiration. Why not use the rib tip to build a brow bone? That evening, he proudly showed me where he had placed a "beam," as he called it, running along her eyebrow line on the crushed side of her face. In the semidarkness of her hospital room, all I could see was one more seeping incision on a small, swollen face full of scars and sutures. But this ridge of bone would not only offer some protection in the event of a blow to the head; it would also give Brenda's forehead a more natural contour, once the swelling had gone down.

Brenda didn't care about any such details that evening as she dozed fretfully in the ICU, oft-wakened by pain, nausea, and the baby crying in the next cubicle. Between moans, she asked me to sing. Nothing came to mind except the praise songs we sang at mealtimes. I put my lips close to her ear and softly sang, "The steadfast love of the Lord never ceases. His mercies never come to an end. They are new every morning, new every morning. Great is thy faithfulness, Oh Lord; great is thy faithfulness!" I got choked up and tearful as I squeaked out the last few words. Looking at this suffering child, I could hardly hold back the thought, *What kind of mercy is this?* I sniffed, and a couple of tears fell on Brenda's pillow. She opened her eye wide and looked at me in surprise; she had never seen me cry. "What's the matter, Mom?" she croaked.

"Oh, honey, I wish there were something I could do to make you feel better," I answered.

Never one to let an opportune moment pass, Brenda closed her eye, paused momentarily, and whispered, "Let me get my ears pierced."

Within a couple of weeks, Brenda had recovered, and her swelling had gone down sufficiently for the promised ear piercing. She had long been begging for this (as if she hadn't been pierced enough already), so it was a happy day for her, and she bravely endured the momentary sting while Kate held her hands. Her energy level and appetite quickly returned to normal. Her biggest irritation was that Dr. Stroncek had placed her on a soft diet, which ruled out meat, pizza, cookies, and several other favorites. She marked the days until her soft diet would end, three weeks after surgery, on July 27. I couldn't bring myself to tell her that therapy was scheduled to resume the very next day, July 28.

With restrictions on her activities, Brenda could not enjoy the outdoor fun of summertime. Biking, skateboarding, and swimming were all prohibited. So she took to collecting caterpillars instead. She would keep them in jars throughout the day, and each evening, we would release the day's catch. She made much of saying good night to them all, even giving some of them bedtime kisses. Meanwhile, our berry patch was producing a bumper crop, and raspberries were a soft food which Brenda loved and could eat to her heart's content. With bumper crops of raspberries come bumper crops of raspberry beetles. Rose and Kate swore off raspberries after a couple of tiny beetles surfaced in the cream they had just poured over their berries one evening. Bob and I tried to reason with them, assuring them that they had probably already eaten several of the harmless, three-millimeter insects which hide deep inside the fresh berries. To prove my point, I picked up one of the tiny beetles, popped it in my mouth, and chugged it down with a gulp of coffee. At first, the girls could hardly believe what I had done, but soon they were passing me their beetles. Brenda, not to be outdone, announced that she had eaten some of her caterpillars: "I ate 151 of them for a snack," she declared. I looked at her with a shocked and dubious expression. "It's okay. They're soft!" she crowed, and laughed hilariously.

Chapter 6

✦

Brenda resumed therapy on July 28, with an appointment in the occupational therapy clinic. Though neither of us wanted to return to the daily torture regimen, we weren't going to let it ruin our summer. There was something exciting in the works; we were planning the biggest camping trip we had ever taken. Bob had narrowed down a list of possible destinations and put them before the family. I'm not sure what swayed the girls as Bob read descriptions of campgrounds and local attractions. Perhaps it was the daily pancake breakfast in the Cody campground, but in the end, "Wyomee," as the younger kids called it, got a unanimous vote, and we began packing.

Perhaps every father dreams of taking his family on a western odyssey. Perhaps most moms are less adventurous. Whenever I expressed apprehension about the long journey with five kids, Bob assured me that the car trip would be leisurely and enjoyable, so broken up by stops at local sites, we would hardly notice that our destination was 1,200 miles from home. I got my first inkling of his true itinerary when he suggested that we leave at 4:30 a.m. on Saturday, August 1.

I was dreading the early departure, but in fact. it was pleasant. Five tousled, bleary-eyed girls stumbled to the van and settled down with their pillows to resume their interrupted sleep. As the sun began to bathe the landscape in its first rosy light, the car was quiet, except for Bob's voice sharing nostalgic memories of childhood travels and the college summers he spent as a cross-country truck driver.

I had packed supplies for picnic breakfasts and lunches at roadside rest areas. When we stopped for each meal, Bob carried the cooler from the van, and I spread our tablecloth and a couple dozen items from the cooler while the kids visited the restrooms. When they returned, Bob quickly assembled his meal and began eating while I helped Rose and Brenda. I then prepared my own plate and was just about to take my first bite when Bob stood up and started packing. "Time to hit the road," he announced with relish, as the girls and I quickly ate what remained on our plates or carried our food to the car.

After lunch the first day, I took the matter up with him. "You said it would be a leisurely trip," I scolded, "and now you're out to break some personal land-speed record." He laughed and told me I was "so cute," but he also relaxed his pace a bit. We had a wonderful afternoon, walking at a Missouri River overlook, visiting the Corn Palace, and driving through the Badlands.

South Dakota is rife with tourist "opportunities." We passed billboards for reptile gardens, caves, pioneer villages, and the infamous Wall Drug. After supper, we visited a prairie dog town.

I looked askance as Bob purchased several small bags of peanuts for fifty cents each from a ramshackle gift shop located next to an acre of dirt mounds. I muttered something about diddling away our vacation budget. I could have purchased *all* those peanuts for *less* than fifty cents at my grocery superstore back home, I pointed out.

"If you could just accept the fact that it's nothing but a tourist trap," Bob counseled me, "you'd probably enjoy it." He was right. I grudgingly accepted the bag of peanuts he offered and found that it was actually fun to feed the little varmints. The girls ran around with glee while Bob bought another round of peanuts and shot half a roll of film.

We finished the day at Wall Drug, where Bob, oh-so-generous with his quarters, ran every animated gadget from the piano-playing gorilla to the shyster peddling snake oil. "Does this drug store actually have a pharmacy?" I asked as we wandered through its enormity. We stayed at this quarter-sucking playground until closing time and then settled down in a small motel cabin in Wall, only blocks from the drug store. By this time, it was after 10 p.m., and since we had risen at 3:30 a.m., we had no trouble falling asleep after a very full day.

The next morning, Bob roused the girls easily by announcing breakfast at the Wall Drug cafe in half an hour. I was jaded to piano-playing gorillas, roaring dinosaurs, and rocking Jackalopes; but for the girls, it was like seeing it all over again for the first time. They were in a jocular mood as we hit the road. After a stop at Mount Rushmore, we began the long haul of the day. ("Long haul" is a trucking term which Bob used with great pleasure.) The monotony of the local scenery was enlivened by our colorful traveling companions— bikers by the hundreds headed for the annual Harley Davidson rally in Sturgis, which 400,000 were expected to attend. Some rode their bikes: male in front, biker babe in back, halter tops, leather chaps, the ubiquitous black scarf. Others drove pickups or motor homes, their gleaming custom Harleys on trailers behind them like little gods.

Squabbles were inevitable as the hours stretched on. I put the girls on a rotating seating chart, changing their places every few hours to give everyone a chance in the most coveted seats while providing relief from tiresome seatmates. I thought things might get out of control during that part of the day when Rose, Kate, and Brenda were lined up beside each other; but the three kept themselves busy in a relatively benign fashion. For part of the day, they played a game called "Two-faced Mom." Kate played the mother of two children: on the favorite she lavished love and devotion, but the other was a scapegoat who received nothing but tongue-lashings and an occasional mock slap. First, Kate would turn toward Brenda with a sickly sweet voice: "Yes, darling, what is it, honey? Tell Mommy what's wrong. Oh, you want that dolly you saw in the catalog? Well, of course you can have it. It only costs four hundred dollars. Come on, sweetie, we'll order it right now."

All the while Kate was talking to Brenda, Rose patted her arm and called, "Mommy, Mommy!" Suddenly, Kate would turn on Rose with a harsh, raspy voice. "What'd'ya want, ya little creep?" she would yell. "If you don't find that welfare check you lost, I'll break both your legs. Now get me my cigarettes. I feel like havin' a smoke." Though I found this game amusing, a parent does wonder where such play comes from: Could it be something I've done? As any parent could predict, their game became progressively physical, and when I heard Kate yell, "Wait a minute. My braces are stuck to your shirt!" I had to call an end to it.

Howdy, pardner… Brenda aboard her trail
horse, Newt, in Cody, Wyoming

On Monday, August 3, we set up camp in Cody, Wyoming, a tourist Mecca in the midst of a barren land. The town's Wild West theme appealed to cowboy wannabes, as well as Midwestern dudes and dudettes like us. There was no end of entertainment for tourists: trail rides, a rodeo, river rafting, a Wild West shoot-out, museums, and a buffalo ranch. Determined to do it all, Bob set about mentally planning our itinerary for the week. The high point would be our day at Yellowstone National Park, fifty-three miles from Cody. Bob was antsy as we waited in line for free pancakes that morning. *What's the rush?* I wondered. *We've got the whole day.*

Though Bob and I enjoyed the breathtaking scenery of Yellowstone, for the girls, it was just another day in the car. We upheld a tradition as old as the automobile, maybe as old as the wagon train: parent points out rugged mountain scene or serene valley; children lift heads briefly, grunt in a ho-hum way and return to their books or Gameboys. Whenever we announced a stop, such as the Paint Pots or Old Faithful, the girls inevitably asked the one all-important question: "Do they have a gift shop?"

The day stretched on, and with a new awareness of the enormity of Yellowstone, I began to see why Bob had hoped for an early start. "Are we out of the park yet?" Brenda asked with irritating regularity. Having failed to plan for delays of various sorts, we ended up leaving by the northeast entrance much later than expected. Soon, darkness fell. There was nothing to light our way except a full moon; reflectors along the road; and our headlights, which somehow seemed much weaker out there in the middle of nowhere. *Fifty-three miles*, I thought. *We should be back at camp in an hour.* Little did I know what Chief Joseph Scenic Highway would be like: a winding mountain road of switchbacks and drop-offs that may be scenic in daylight, but at night, I found it all quite nerve-wracking. Signs along the way did not calm me: Rough Road, Dip, Bump, Extreme Rough Road, No Shoulder, Drop Off, Slide Zone, Watch for Fallen Rock, Game Crossing Next 3 Miles, Open Range, Stock on Road.

Deer and beef cattle on the shoulder, suddenly illumined by our headlights, unnerved me; but Bob was ever steady at the wheel and seemed to draw some perverse enjoyment from this driving challenge. Thankfully, we arrived at camp safe and sound, though not until 11:30 p.m. Everyone was exhausted, and I expected even Brenda to sleep well. So far, she had slept poorly in the tent, thrashing about and sometimes sitting up or talking in her sleep. She would wriggle out of her blankets, and since Cody was cold at night, hypothermia was a legitimate concern. Taking all these factors into consideration, I resolved to sleep with Brenda each night and keep her covered. After our day at Yellowstone, I slept soundly until 3 a.m., when I woke with a feeling that something was amiss. I strained my eyes in the darkness to check on Brenda, but Brenda was nowhere to be found. I patted the blankets next to me—nothing. When I had peered all around the tent and didn't see her, I began to panic. A scene from childhood leaped into my mind: flashlight beams dancing on the walls of our canvas tent and men's voices calling the name of a toddler who had disappeared at our lakeside campground in the middle of the night. Thankfully, that little boy had been found sleeping peacefully in a nest of leaves beside a wooded path. But what about Brenda? Had she also wandered off in her sleep?

Stay calm, I counseled myself. Wriggling out of my blankets, I moved around the tent, patting the beds and the floor between our inflatable mattresses. What a relief to feel a curled-up form peacefully sleeping at Rose's feet, completely covered by blankets. I decided not to disturb the little mole since she was well bundled. I lay down reassured, but it was at least an hour before I slept again.

At 7:30 the next morning, Bob called reveille. He had made reservations for our family to tour a buffalo ranch in just one hour. I was beginning to feel the strain of our active schedule and the difference in Bob's and my ideas of vacation. Bob considered our tent a base camp from which to explore the area. I preferred a more leisurely pace, with time to wander along mountain paths, gaze at stars in the night sky, linger beside the campfire, roast marshmallows, and chat about nothing. When I broached the subject with Bob, he again told me I was "so cute," but he also agreed to spend some time at camp that day. The girls went swimming while I did laundry, and that evening, we grilled buffalo burgers over the campfire, finishing our meal with s'mores.

The rest of the week passed at a more leisurely pace. The weather was good, the kids made friends in the campground, and we watched fellow campers come and go, many of them one-nighters on Harleys. Just when Bob and I were starting to feel like relaxed vacationers, it was time to break camp and start for home. Since part of our route paralleled the Oregon Trail, our journey was dotted with remembrances of the pioneers. Predictably, the girls were not as moved as their parents by wagon-wheel ruts preserved in Wyoming sandstone, but if nothing else, it was a good chance for them to stretch their legs. They romped and ran, oblivious in the shadow of Registry Rock, a large sandstone face in the Platte Valley, where resting pioneers had the leisure to carve their names and dates while their stock enjoyed a few days' reprieve before their arduous mountain crossing. I felt the presence of heroes there. *How little we can imagine*, I thought, *of the difficulties courageous immigrants faced on the trail.* Of course,

I sympathized with the women whose experience would have made our camping trip seem like a picnic.

For the girls, the trip home stretched on and on, punctuated by Brenda's question after almost every stop: "By the way, are we almost there?" August 11 was our last day of travel, and we opted for the old highway rather than the dull interstate. As we traveled through Iowa farmland and small towns, I reviewed the trip in my own mind. We had traveled almost 3,300 miles—an average of 300 miles a day. We would arrive home a little weary, a little wiser, and a little more appreciative of this vast country we lived in. I reflected on the many faces we had seen: the shaded faces of real-life cowboys, the massive faces of buffalo, the scarf-topped faces of bikers, the smiling faces of pancake cooks at our campground, the rock faces of four famous presidents, and the sandstone face of a less formal but equally meaningful monument. That evening, as we pulled into our own driveway, we were all relieved to see the cheerful face of our own little house on Browning Road. There's nothing like camping to make you appreciate your own bed. There's nothing like public restrooms to make you appreciate your own hot shower. There's nothing like a few nights in a motel to make you appreciate the privacy of your own home. We turned on central air and sank gratefully into a long, deep sleep.

Chapter 7

W hen school resumed, our morning routine—and life in general—was considerably eased by Noli's absence. Grace began her second year of high school, Laura and Kate were middle schoolers, Rose was in third grade, and Brenda was in second. For Rose, who had struggled with reading, phonics suddenly clicked, and she took to reading like a kid to cotton candy. Who would have thought that Bob and I, two college English majors, would ever consider putting limits on a child's reading time? But reading was all Rose wanted to do. As soon as her homework was finished each afternoon, she curled up on the couch and traveled far away into the book she was currently devouring. Her sisters' invitations and pleas to join in their play fell on deaf ears. One day, when Kate couldn't convince, cajole, or bribe Rose away from her book, she finally shouted in anger, "You used to be a *good* sister, before you learned to read!"

During one of Brenda's recheck appointments that fall, Dr. Hardy told us that he planned to operate in December—Brenda's last surgery during this stay. Grace had come along that day, and as we walked through the hospital corridors after the appointment, she said, "I've been in this building so many times I could find my way around with my eyes closed."

"Yup," I answered, "this certainly is Brenda's home away from home."

"You mean," Grace corrected me, "her home away from home away from home."

This reminder of Brenda's impending departure saddened me. But we knew by now that this visit, which would soon end, was only phase one of a long, involved project. Brenda would make frequent return trips to Madison for reconstructive surgery and therapy; she would be a child with two homes, two families, and two countries.

Brenda continued the intense therapy regimen she had resumed in late July, but it resulted in little progress. Dr. Stroncek believed that the jaw joint he had made was functional. The culprit was a strong band of scar tissue, about the size of his pinky finger, on the injured side of her mouth. We could not see this band, because it was under her skin. But I could feel it when I put my gloved fingers into her mouth during therapy sessions. The pull of the band was so strong that Brenda was unable to bite down, close her teeth, or chew effectively. The only cure would be to cut the band, but until that could be done during the December operation, we would try to maintain the limited jaw mobility she had gained. One night, as I sat beside her at the dinner table, she asked if I could hear her crunching her corn chips.

Hmmmm, I wondered, not for the first time, *how does she chomp on corn chips, anyway?* "Chew those with your lips open," I ordered, and as she happily obliged, I peered into her mouth. Brenda had found a way to masticate her food, though for the life of me, I couldn't figure out how. I turned my attention back to my own dinner.

"Not very interesting in there, is it," she commented blandly, popping another chip into her mouth.

It was a charmed autumn in Madison. We savored warm breezes, sunshine, and brilliant fall colors, unaware that a storm was brewing in Brenda's homeland. At the beginning of November, Hurricane Mitch stalled over Central America, devastating the landscape and ravaging the idyllic Trujillo, Brenda's hometown. We took pains to shield Brenda from the news, muting television reports and warning our daughters to say nothing about it. I called Brenda's teacher to let her know that Brenda was unaware of the destruction and the rising death toll caused by Mitch, the worst hurricane on record. Our faxes to Trujillo failed to go through, and we could learn nothing about the welfare of Brenda's family for days. "I bet the blue piano is gone," Bob said sadly after the radio news one morning.

At last, we received a call from Sonia, Brenda's adult half sister in Michigan. She passed along a grapevine report that, though her mother's home and beachside bar had been completely washed away by the driving wind and rain, the family was unharmed. Bolstered by this relatively good news, I decided to tell Brenda about the hurricane. I took her in her bedroom, closed the door, wrapped my arms around her, and delivered the news. She passively received the report on her family. When I told her about the destruction of her home, she was not perturbed. Her only comment was that her papa should be safe because the town jail was built of bricks. Then, to my surprise, she informed me that she had heard about the hurricane days earlier. "What exactly did you hear?" I asked.

"That there was a real bad storm in Honduras and lots of people were dead," she said in a matter-of-fact tone.

"Weren't you worried?" I asked. "Why didn't you say something?"

"Because I forgot all about it," she answered with a shrug. "Can I go now?"

My concern shifted from the devastation in Brenda's home country to the microclimate of her mind and heart. What accounted for the sea change that was so evident? Perhaps the physical elements of her other life were too remote now to matter, but her disregard for her mother and family surprised me. Her sense of belonging now seemed centered in *our* home and family; the ties to her birth family had weakened during the long months she had been away from her rightful home. Trujillo was a distant memory that stirred no passion.

In truth, the Caribbean resort community was a tranquil paradise, but Brenda's life there had not been. After a scanty breakfast (maybe), her mother turned the children loose to flit among tourists, begging and fending for themselves the rest of the day. What would it be like for an Americanized child to return to her third-world life—a life of uncertainty, poverty, curious stares, and beggary—an even more impoverished life now that her mother was destitute? A wave of regret washed over me. We had created a child with one foot in each of two very different cultures. Could she be truly happy and well-adjusted in either home?

And on a purely practical note, who in Trujillo would have the time or energy to keep up with Brenda's therapy and preserve her hard-won jaw function? This wasn't the first time I had fretted over such worries. I presumed that Brenda's daily regimen would be near the bottom of her mother's list of priorities—somewhere below scrabbling for something to eat, keeping her children in clothes, and locating a domicile.

The worsening reports from Honduras and Nicaragua weighed heavily on me as the days passed, and more so as I worried about former foster children who lived in towns that were wiped out by the devastating storm. Hurricane Mitch's death toll rose to nine or ten thousand, with thousands still missing. In Nicaragua, raging floods washed out entire communities. Rescue crews venturing into mountain villages climbed high into tall trees to retrieve children whose parents had tied them with ropes to upper branches. The rescued children wandered about confused, unclaimed, and separated from parents, many of whom had died. In cities, refugees gathered in shelters or huddled in pelting rain, unable to find food or warmth. Survivors were besieged by infection after days spent in mud and dirty water. People sat in a daze, their glazed eyes trying to take in the unfamiliar landscape and the tragedy that had befallen them. The dead were so numerous they were being buried by earth-moving equipment. "We will never really know how many have died," a Nicaraguan official said.

How was Brenda's mother coping with this catastrophe? I wondered. Where was she staying? Was she alone, or surrounded by a chaos of miserable refugees? Did the future seem hopeless, or did she cherish a dream that she would rebuild and start over? Had she walked along the beach where her little home and business used to be? I supposed that everything manmade must be gone, except perhaps some debris. No house. No bar. No blue piano. Only one thing was the same—the waves washing up on the sand, just as they always had.

In contrast, our own lovely weather continued right through Thanksgiving weekend. We took walks in our shirtsleeves, and that Saturday, we enjoyed a picnic lunch on our patio. The girls rode their bikes and played in the park across the street. All but Grace. A doll-making kit she had ordered arrived in the most timely fashion on Friday morning, so it could just as well be seventeen degrees below zero as far as she was concerned. She was busy in the house with her needle and thread.

Perhaps it was the crafting of a new doll that put Kate in mind of the long-forgotten Baby Alive. From the bottom of a toy box in the basement, she resurrected her specimen of this quintessentially American phenomenon—a plastic baby that eats, urinates, and (yes, I'm afraid so) defecates. After a considerable amount of pleading and persuasion from Kate, I dug out the recipe for Baby Alive food. While Kate went in search of two C batteries, I made a concoction of cornstarch, gelatin, water, and green food coloring. Kate and Brenda waited anxiously while the mixture cooked and cooled. At last, Baby Alive's strained peas were ready. Amid high excitement, the doll began ingesting her spoon-fed meal atop the kitchen table. Satisfied that all was going well, I (foolishly) left the room. About ten minutes later, I returned and started putting away plates that had dried in the open dishwasher.

"Careful, Mom," warned Grace, serenely seated nearby, sewing her doll. "There might be strained peas on those... Oh, and on the phone and maybe on the calendar and probably on the cupboard doors over there." A story soon unfolded which accounted for the uproarious laughter I had heard during my brief absence. When Baby Alive's intake became a little too sluggish to suit Kate, she headed to the bathroom closet, where several large syringes were stored. These syringes, now bath toys, had been used to feed Brenda during recent hospitalizations. Certainly not the first baby to balk at strained peas, Baby Alive was about to have them orally injected by force. But when Kate's grip on the syringe slipped, strained peas took to the air, flying over the counter and landing on the far side of the kitchen. I decided it was time to end the feeding session, and removed Baby Alive's batteries so I could wash the strained peas off her body and out of her hair.

"Baby Alive is going back to inactive status," I told Kate, putting the two batteries in my pocket.

"What?!" she cried, "you mean my baby is *dead*?"

"Dead as a doornail," I answered. "Definitely too dead to eat or poop." Baby Alive's day in the sun was over, and soon she would return to a dark corner of the basement for another three or four years of neglect.

Brenda, who had now been with us for eighteen months, was not sorry to spend a second Christmas in the United States. Her final surgery was scheduled for the week before Christmas.

Dr. Hardy was sure she would recover in time for our trip to Michigan to spend the holiday with Bob's parents and family as planned. Brenda was carefree during the busy Christmas season, enjoying class parties, school programs, gift exchanges, and high excitement of all sorts.

Surgery day began very early in the morning as a sleepy Brenda stumbled to the bathtub. "You look tired," I said sympathetically.

"I am," she answered. "Good thing I get to sleep all day."

Dr. Hardy looked a little like the cat that ate the canary when he joined me for the usual postoperative chat that afternoon. I shared his pride and pleasure. He had just brought to fruition phase one of the plans and dreams he began formulating the very first time he met Brenda. Whatever else Brenda might receive for Christmas, I knew that his gift—her vastly improved appearance—was the best of them all.

I felt a twinge of apprehension, however, when he told me that our departure to Michigan might be delayed. As usual, Brenda's surgery had been longer and more involved than planned, and thus she would need more time to recover. That night, Bob called his parents to explain. They were disappointed but understanding. What choice did we have?

The days passed and Brenda improved, but slowly. When December 24 dawned and she was still in the hospital, all hopes of Christmas with Bob's family evaporated. As I arrived in pediatrics that morning, I saw one of Dr. Hardy's students at the nurse's station. I stopped by for a chat, hoping to put in a word for Brenda's departure. When he uttered the magic word, *discharge*, I said, "The sooner, the better!" but I held out little hope. I knew all too well the many ways a hospital discharge can stall out as those involved consult with each other, visit the patient, perform interviews and examinations, prescribe medications, and finally sign on the dotted line.

To my utter amazement, a nurse appeared in Brenda's room five minutes later with discharge papers. I quickly looked them over, signed them, and ran off to the hospital pharmacy to pick up her prescriptions. When I returned a few minutes later, a pediatric resident was examining her. He had been following her throughout her hospitalization, but he seemed unaware that she was officially discharged. He expressed concern over her appetite (or lack thereof) and failure to produce solid waste. "What sort of a diet is she on right now?" he asked.

"Full liquids," I answered.

"We'll have to see how she does with meals today," he said. I smiled and nodded, hoping Brenda wouldn't spill the beans. Personally, I wasn't the least concerned about her digestion, knowing from experience that going home would be the best tonic and she would soon produce her big poop of the day.

Bob's parents' home in Michigan, where we were wined, dined, and pampered

The aforementioned resident notwithstanding, I absconded with Dr. Hardy's little patient at the first possible moment, arriving home at about 9:30 a.m., to the delight of the whole family. The next two hours were a flurry of excited packing and scurrying about. "Are my khaki pants washed?" "Where are my dress shoes?" "Don't forget socks and underpants!" "Can I have some gift wrap?" "Who took the Scotch Tape?" "Did you pack my shaver?" We pulled out of the driveway at noon. At least, it was noon the first time. There were several returns to the house for forgotten essentials. Pulling out of the driveway on our fifth attempt, Bob looked at the odometer and commented in a droll voice, "Eight miles, and we haven't left our own neighborhood." I willfully turned off the frantic last-minute review going on in my mind. *We're not going back again*, I told myself. *Whatever we've forgotten, we'll have to get by without.* Surprisingly, we had every truly essential item, and we pulled into Bob's parents' driveway right at dinnertime. The aroma of simmering beef roast filled the house. Christmas lights twinkled, a fire crackled on the hearth, and carols played softly in the background. Grandpa had made Shirley Temples for all his "grandbabies," and for us adults, glasses of wine gleamed in the soft light of the living room. I sank into an overstuffed chair and let the whirlwind of the past few days drift from my mind.

Chapter 8

The holidays were like a peaceful oasis. Shortly after we returned home from Michigan, my parents arrived, and so did deep snow and extreme cold. The house felt cozy, warm, and happy that Friday as we welcomed the New Year with a festive holiday dinner. Saturday morning, we woke to blizzard conditions, and the girls gazed out the windows in a forlorn mood. A Saturday trip to the mall with Grandma was a mainstay of every visit, and they knew this was the only weekend Grandma would be with us. I told them repeatedly not to get their hopes up: the weather was too severe to go out for anything less than a life-threatening medical emergency. That afternoon, to my surprise, Bob suggested that we bundle up; he would drive us to the mall. It's hard to believe now that we actually risked life and limb on snow-covered roads, in zero visibility, to go shopping. There was something about severe driving conditions that Bob, the former trucker, couldn't resist. He was steady at the wheel throughout that long five-mile trip. When my dad, who had come along to help shovel and push if needed, walked us from the car to the mall entrance, we learned that the mall was closing due to the severe weather. The girls handled the disappointment admirably; and we returned to our home, where we could observe the wintry weather in warmth and comfort—the only way to watch a blizzard, in my opinion. That evening during dinner, the phone rang: the next day's church service was cancelled. Bob raised his glass "to being snowed in." Perhaps we should have felt worse about the cancellation, but we were so cozy and contented that another whole day of the same sounded most agreeable.

The girls hoped for a cancellation on Monday as well; but by that time, the roads were clear, and Christmas vacation ended on schedule. We plunged back into carpooling, homework, music lessons, therapy appointments, and clinic visits. At a postsurgical follow-up appointment that week, Dr. Hardy admired his own handiwork, smiling as he turned Brenda this way and that. "You look great," he said with satisfaction.

"You did all the work," she quipped. "All I did was take a nap."

Like most people who seriously engage in a hobby, I wanted something to show for my efforts of the past year. When the totals were in, I chalked up seventy-five medical and dental appointments. Thirty of those were Brenda's. I had taken children to fifteen kinds of medical professionals, including a neurologist, orthopedic surgeon, orthodontist, ophthalmologist, speech pathologist, plastic surgeon, oral surgeon, cardiologist, and craniofacial surgeon. Though medical appointments were not my favorite activity, at every visit, I learned something new—and I don't mean the latest gossip from *People* magazine, though Lord knows I paged through enough of those in waiting rooms.

Except for therapy, the doctors had finished their work on Brenda. After we were given a tentative date of February 20 for her return to Trujillo, I began the difficult process of letting go. Predominant among my many concerns was fear that without consistent therapy, Brenda would lose the jaw mobility she had worked so hard to gain. I planned to send video of a therapy session and careful instructions for every aspect of Brenda's regimen. Yet I knew that her mother faced much more pressing issues than making sure Brenda maintained at least 26 millimeters of mobility.

One day, Bob, who worked for a seed company, brought a large box of seed packets home from the office and asked if I would deliver them to the surgery clinic on one of our trips to the hospital. Dr. Doyle, an oral surgeon and an associate of Dr. Hardy, had asked Bob for a donation of garden seed which his team could distribute to locals during an upcoming medical mission trip to a third-world country. (Providing seeds is the same link through which Bob was acquainted with Dr. Schumaker, whose medical team had discovered Brenda on a mission trip to Trujillo.) At Brenda's next appointment, I asked a nurse where I could leave the box for Dr. Doyle. "He's sitting in that room over there," she said. "Why don't you give it to him yourself?"

We had never met Dr. Doyle, who happened to be the chief of the Dentistry Section at UW Hospital and director of the Temporomandibular Joint Disorder Clinic, with a special interest in facial trauma cases. (The temporomandibular joints are the complex hinging and sliding joints connecting the jawbone to the skull.)

"So this is Brenda," he said in a kind voice, and it was obvious that he was familiar with her case. "Come and let me look at you." He peered into her mouth, then turned her head and looked at her jaw. We talked about what had been done and the therapy that was vital to the success of Brenda's rebuilt jaw. In veiled language, I shared my concern that Brenda's daily regimen might fall by the wayside when she returned to Trujillo. Dr. Doyle turned Brenda's head from side to side and ordered her to open and close her mouth. "Hmmm… I wonder if I could make a device that she can insert by herself," Dr. Doyle thought aloud. "In that case, she could maintain her own mobility without relying on an adult to do therapy with her. Can you stay long enough to get some X-rays taken?" he asked.

"No problem," I replied, struggling to keep my tone casual and stifling a sudden urge to turn cartwheels, shout for joy, kneel before him, and kiss his hand repeatedly. I would have stayed the rest of the day—the rest of the week!—for the sake of such a prospect. What a wish come true! To think that we had, seemingly by accident, met the very man who could put my worries to rest and give Brenda the power to preserve the millimeters she had worked, cried, sweated, and bled for during the past thirteen months!

That very afternoon, Dr. Doyle ordered X-rays and took molds of Brenda's mouth. Within a few days, her custom-made appliance would be ready, and there would still be time to work out the bugs before she left Madison. Brenda seemed oblivious to her good fortune. I tried to describe the importance of her new device, but her eye glazed over. To her, it was just one more appliance contrived by one more doctor and presented at one more appointment in a long, long string of appointments.

February 20 crept closer, and with it, Brenda's inevitable departure. We had said goodbye to many foster children before, but none of them had been with us for such a long time. We didn't speak of it, but I knew that each family member was dreading the sad days when we would feel her abrupt absence so keenly. In my own mind, I began the process of letting go my investment in her therapy. I knew I had to stop fretting and place the future of Brenda's jaw in the hands of her mother and herself.

Just then, we received a fax from Brenda's mother, who was still struggling to get back on her feet after the devastation wrought by Hurricane Mitch. If it wasn't too much trouble, she asked, could we keep Brenda for two additional months? I quickly responded: Yes, we would gladly keep her a bit longer. Suddenly, the world looked brighter. Two more months to fight that scar tissue! Two more months of healing and stretching would make success almost certain, I was sure. My surge of optimism was confirmed at our next hospital therapy session when, for the first time ever, Brenda measured 30 millimeters of jaw mobility. At last, we were gaining the victory!

However, scar tissue is a formidable and capricious opponent. With immense disappointment, I watched Brenda's mobility decrease over the next few weeks. The familiar pattern was mysteriously repeating itself. I started to notice more resistance at therapy time; everything felt a little tighter, despite Brenda's deep-breathing efforts to relax. Even the professionals, with all their training and specialized devices, couldn't maintain the mobility we had achieved. After an hour of strenuous therapy in the clinic, Brenda's mobility measured at 29 millimeters, and the next week 27, and then 25.

Brenda was the picture of cooperation, and even suggested her own ideas for stretching and maintaining, which her therapists, who were creative problem solvers, often tried. We used Dr. Doyle's custom device, as well as shims and wedges of every size and shape; but her scar tissue was stronger than any feasible method we could come up with. Though it seemed that modern medical technology should be able to triumph over a few bands of flesh, we were losing the third round in this war on my personal enemy—Brenda's scar tissue.

Brenda never chose to give up. It was her drive to overcome that fueled my own. She was indomitable. As we traveled across town to yet another painful therapy session, she would be carefree, reading aloud a chapter book from school as I occasionally helped out with an unfamiliar word or a phrase she didn't know. "Worn to a...," she said one day, stumbling over the text. I glanced over as she held up the book with furrowed brow.

"A frazzle," I said. She looked at me, mystified. "You know, worn to a frazzle—completely exhausted or stressed out," I explained.

"Worn to a frazzle," she repeated, enjoying the sound of this new idiom.

Later, after an hour of excruciating therapy, Brenda threw herself into the passenger seat of the van and sighed heavily.

"You seem tired," I observed solicitously.

She wiped her brow dramatically. "I'm worn to a fuzzy," she said.

With the extension of her stay came the second birthday Brenda would celebrate in the United States—her eighth. As I tucked her into bed beside Rose on the eve of her special day, I prayed aloud that her far-away twin sister, Abigail, would have a fine birthday celebration the next day in Trujillo. When the prayer was over, Brenda said, "I don't think Abigail will have a good birthday."

"Why wouldn't she?" I asked, surprised.

"Because," Brenda answered sadly, "people in Trujillo don't know that it's their birthday."

The next day, Brenda arrived home from school eager to show me the birthday surprise she had chosen from a treasure trove her teacher kept in the classroom: a cheap metal ring with a red plastic "gem" the diameter of a dime. With great fanfare, she withdrew the treasured jewel from her pocket, only to find that the stone had fallen out of the setting. She tearfully retrieved the stone, and I promised to remount it. But I found that this was no easy task, partly because I lacked the proper tools and partly because the gem was in fact too large for the prongs that were supposed to hold it.

Drying her tears, I fell back on my usual contingency: "Show it to Dad when he gets home. I'm sure he can fix it." She waited eagerly for his arrival, flinging herself and her damaged jewel into his arms as he walked through the door. I'm not sure how fathers feel when, after a long day at the office, they're greeted on the doorstep by a distressed child and a repair job. But for Bob that evening, jewelry repair was Job One, and with the delicate modeling tools in his basement workshop, the task was soon accomplished. Brenda reappeared ten minutes later, the flashy jewel on her finger upstaged only by the relief and joy on her face.

This ring became her constant adornment, and she was wearing it a few days later when we took a picnic lunch to a local park. As Brenda skipped off toward the playground, I followed with trepidation. For her sake, I dreaded the stares and questions that invariably occurred when other children encountered her for the first time. To her, this rite of passage was a mere annoyance; if she was self-conscious about her appearance, she refused to show it. She was businesslike but not rude, answering queries briefly and in a matter-of-fact way. As I stood nearby that day, a half circle of curious kids gathered around Brenda.

"What happened to your face?" A girl of about her own age asked the inevitable question.

"I got hit by a truck," Brenda answered.

"Where did your eye go?" the child wondered.

"It got wrecked in the accident," Brenda replied.

The little girl studied Brenda's features for a moment, deep in thought. "Well, I have two eyes, and you only have one," she said, reaching for Brenda's bejeweled hand. "But you have that pretty ring on your finger, and I don't have any ring at all." After this proclamation declaring the two girls even, they clasped hands and ran off to play.

Such conversations with strangers were unavoidable. I could not deny that Brenda's face was still a curiosity; her scars would always be obvious. But her appearance was much improved. Her hair was back where it should be, on top of her head instead of covering a quarter of her face. Gone were the weeping bald spot, the caved-in eye socket, and sinus fluids dripping from a hole in her cheek. Her facial contours were almost normal, and the damage no longer distorted her expression of the winsome joy within. She had a new confidence among her peers.

And now that her scalp wounds had healed, she took new interest in her hair. She carefully brushed and combed it each morning, then tied it back in a ponytail or "bun." These buns looked like little porcupines. Since her hair was short, it was all ends standing out like bristles. Within minutes, at least half of her hair would escape completely, but she seemed oblivious and proudly left for school with a bun, just like her big sister Grace. Perhaps her classmates thought she looked ridiculous. Her teachers might wonder why I didn't do something about her hair. Objectively speaking, it was one bad hair day after another. But I couldn't be objective. After everything she had been through, it was gratifying just to see her doing what every little girl does: brushing and primping and standing before the mirror admiring the results of her efforts.

Chapter 9

O n the first evening of my parents' visit that spring, my mother
came into the kitchen and asked in a subdued voice, "Do you
know that Brenda is in the living room jamming a wedge into her
mouth and crying?" Mom may not have seen this as a positive, but
in fact, Brenda's hospital therapists had taught her to manage her
own maintenance therapy and graduated her from their care just a
couple of weeks earlier. Brenda took her therapy as seriously as I
ever had and spared herself no pain. As a result, her mobility held at
26–28 millimeters, and though she couldn't bite into a hamburger
with all the fixin's, she could eat neatly with utensils, brush her teeth,
and enjoy near-normal mouth function. I was gratefully decommis-
sioned. But I was also painfully aware that there was no reason to keep
Brenda any longer. I was waiting for a phone call I didn't want—the
one in which the local Healing the Children director would give me
Brenda's departure date.

The flexible wedge that Dr. Doyle had fashioned worked well,
and after a bit of practice, Brenda was able to insert it without difficulty. However, it cracked every few weeks. Then it was Bob to the
rescue: a little filing, a little model glue; and Brenda was back in business. This was the kind of bothersome detail that worried me. *Who
in Trujillo is gonna glue this thing back together?* I would ask myself as
I handed the cracked appliance to Bob.

He encouraged me not to fret about Brenda's home going.
When I tossed and turned during the night, he would take me in
his arms and assure me that things were going to work out. But he
knew that, in addition to my concern about logistical details, my
heart was heavy over the thought of life without Brenda. Determined
to distract me, at least for one evening, Bob made secret plans for

our eighteenth wedding anniversary. When we arrived at an elegant lakeside seafood restaurant that night, we were shown to a candlelit corner booth, where a lovely vase of roses awaited me. Bob slid into the booth beside me, kissed me, and urged me to let go of my worries for one night. "No talking about the kids," he said gently, "not even Brenda."

I fingered a piece of folded paper in the pocket of my dress. The timing was not quite right, but how could I withhold from my fellow parent, and the love of my life, the faxed message I had received that very day from Trujillo? And so it happened that, by the glow of candlelight, I translated for Bob the letter that had arrived that afternoon—a destitute mother's plea that we adopt her daughter Brenda. Our romantic evening together was spent weighing the ramifications of this monumental request. Such were the sweet nothings we whispered that night.

The challenge of an international adoption, with all its expense and difficulty, loomed large, not to mention the commitment of guiding a disfigured little girl through what promised to be a difficult childhood and adolescence. Yet the alternative—sending her back to a life of poverty, begging, and ridicule—was a bleak prospect and one that we had often wished we had the power to change. This wasn't the first time we'd ever been asked to consider an adoption. But it was the first time that we didn't have the option to say, as we had in some cases, "This child might do better in a different family...a smaller family...a family that can afford the adoption fees." This time, it was us or no one.

We didn't make a decision that night; but for the remainder of the week, we considered, discussed, researched, and prayed about the option to adopt Brenda. Our girls may have wondered why their parents were so distracted, but we said nothing to them about the subject that was on our minds daily. There was no sudden shaft of insight, no sign from God, no clear sense of leading. But over the course of days, the two of us quietly walked apace and arrived at a joint conclusion: we would do it if it could be done.

We knew that the first step—and the proof of her earnest—would be the termination of Brenda's mother's parental rights, a legal action that would need to be solemnized in a Honduran courtroom. We sent funds to cover her legal fees and began the complicated paperwork we would need to submit. Because Brenda had originally come to the United States on a six-month medical visa which had lapsed, she had no legal status; we knew that would complicate and perhaps even jeopardize the process. We asked the office staff of a Wisconsin state senator to help us manage the international communications, and through his staff, we obtained a list of documents that would be required by the Honduran government before an international adoption could be considered. The packet of affidavits, testimonials, and recommendations took weeks to assemble. By the time the task was done, the dog days of summer had set in. It was so "hot and human," as Brenda put it, that outdoor play wasn't very appealing. Laura and Grace had part-time jobs, but aside from that, all five kids were indoors most of every day. It might as well have been January. Boredom set in, and the girls were often on each other's nerves. One evening, they came to supper engaged in an argument about a book they all wanted to read. Grace, who had the coveted item squirreled away in her closet, claimed ownership. While the family gathered at the dinner table, the argument became more and more heated. "Girls," Bob called to them, but they continued their angry discussion. "*Girls*," he said more loudly, but the accusations continued to fly. "*GIRLS!*" he shouted sternly. They looked at him in surprise. Now that he had their attention, he folded his hands and spoke in a quiet voice. "Let's continue this angry dispute after we've asked God to bless our time together at this meal," he suggested.

Summer dragged on, and the girls grew more and more fractious. Thus, I was not in the most receptive mood on a Friday in late July, when we received faxed copies of the legal documents by which Brenda's mother had terminated her parental rights. These papers cleared the way for us to move toward adoption, and on the one hand, I was relieved. On the other hand, it saddened me that a mother's relationship with her own child had to be broken in this way. And at the back of my mind was a nagging concern about how Brenda would take the news. She rarely spoke of her mother, her family, or her hometown; but how would she feel once she knew that her adults had made this momentous decision without consulting her? She would never again run along the warm beaches of Trujillo, live with her mother, or enjoy the apparently large family into which she had been born. Would she be angry or sad or glad that these things would no longer be a part of her life?

As it happened, Bob and I had plans to go out for dinner that Friday evening, a date that was long overdue and had been postponed a couple of times. I was ready to be wined and dined, and was not anxious to discuss our children. Bob, who had not been with them full-time all week, kept bringing up the subject of the kids and particularly the change in Brenda's status. After our server brought a glass of burgundy to accompany his steak, Bob sighed with contentment. "This is great," he said, lifting his glass and smiling. "We have a lot to celebrate."

"Yeah," I said flatly, staring into my glass of water. "It's a girl."

Now that Brenda's mother had signed on the dotted line, we at last felt comfortable telling the girls of our hope that Brenda would soon become a Boomsma. While she played outdoors with some neighbor children that Saturday afternoon, we gathered the other four in the living room for a family meeting. Though I thought Grace had some suspicion of what was coming, she was as surprised as the others, and all were delighted by the idea.

Uncertain what to expect from Brenda, Bob and I sat down with her alone shortly thereafter. He took her on his lap and wrapped his arms around her. I had been thinking for days about how to explain her circumstance. I told her that though her mother loved and missed her, she wasn't able to care for her, in part because of the changes Hurricane Mitch had brought to her life. Besides, I continued, Madison would be the best place for her to receive the ongoing medical care she needed, and her mother wanted to do what was best for her. Admittedly, I was making some of this up since her mother had not actually expressed any of these sentiments. But I could easily put myself in the place of a destitute woman whose home and business—which was only marginal anyway—had been destroyed. So I gave Brenda all the reasons that made it sensible for a mother to do what her mother had done.

It was clear that the possibility of adoption had never occurred to Brenda. She was incredulous at first, but soon a look of relief came over her face. "I'm going to be a Boomsma?" she asked. We both nodded, smiling tentative, hopeful smiles. "Yes! Yes! Yes!" she cried with joy. "I'll always have shoes! I'll never cut my feet on broken glass!" In all our conversations about Brenda's anticipated return to Trujillo, she had never mentioned a single worry about footwear or broken glass, so it seemed odd that this little detail was foremost in her mind. I have since wondered whether grasping at some small reality made our momentous, life-changing announcement more manageable for her.

We promised that her mother would never forget her, that we would keep writing and hope for a reunion someday. But Brenda didn't need our reassurances, because she didn't seem to have any regrets or attachments to Trujillo anymore. We encouraged her to express whatever negative feelings she might have about this new arrangement, but she seemed thoroughly and genuinely pleased. When we excused her, she bounced off Bob's lap and ran to the backyard, where Kate was swimming in our stock-tank swimming pool. Bob and I watched through the window as Brenda and a very wet Kate embraced, laughing and dancing together. Kate shared with Brenda what she remembered of the day we finalized Rose's adoption. "The judge takes his hammer and goes, Bam Bam, 'She's yours.'" I didn't hear this myself, but I knew it had happened when, later that day, I found Brenda dancing and twirling while singing a song she had made up: "I'm gonna be adopted! I'm gonna be adopted when the judge says, 'Bam Bam, She's yours!'"

The summer months flew past. Our trip to Colorado in August was a mixed bag of rain, cloudy weather, and sunshine; quality time with extended family and irritating tight quarters in our van; indescribable mountain vistas; and disappointing tourist traps. Upon returning home, we were all ready to declare it our last family road trip for a while. But within days, the reliable mist of nostalgia descended over my memories, and the less pleasant incidents began to fade. Grace, our indefatigable archivist, was assembling another page of her vacation scrapbook as I worked at the kitchen counter.

"It's hard to say what my favorite part of the trip was," she commented to no one in particular. "The Silverton and Durango train trip was fun. The Royal Gorge was sure beautiful. We had a good time at the Great Sand Dunes. The alligator farm was interesting. Then there was the Garden of the Gods. Hmmm..." She turned to the nearest sister, who happened to be sitting at the computer. "Laura," she asked, "what was your favorite part of the trip?"

Laura answered without hesitating or turning from the screen. "The game room at the campground," she said flatly.

When we arrived home, the start of another school year loomed in the very near future; and one day—seemingly all of a sudden—the girls were gone. The house was quiet and littered with the leavings of summer. Roller blades, helmets, sneakers, and swimsuits lay scattered on bedroom floors. A spare table in the kitchen held Grace's scrapbooking station. I noticed for the first time that Brenda had never turned in her book list for the library's summer reading program. Artifacts from the girls' summer school science course were scattered about: papier-mâché planets, rock-candy cups, grass-top-head characters. During that first week, I reclaimed the house for civilization. At last, order was restored to my world. The hours of each day seemed to stretch out luxuriously without interruption. Projects I had jettisoned over the summer could be resumed. But with all that longed-for order and structure came an emptiness and a marker of time's passing. The beginning of a new school year always reminded me how fleeting the years of childhood are.

And so did an exercise in Grace's Family Financial Management class. Students were paired up as couples and instructed to plan an ersatz wedding and honeymoon, and prepare for the imminent birth of their first child. The girls took to this assignment like ducks to water, hastily nabbing the latest copy of *Modern Bride* magazine from the nearest library or drug store. The boys, in charge of honeymoon planning, did not flock to the nearest travel agency with the same fervor. Grace soon had a presentation notebook started and enjoyed filling it with her selections of dresses, cakes, flowers, and all the other frills and thrills of planning a wedding. When she chose a $200 flower arrangement for the head table at the reception, I suggested that she make the most of this pretend wedding since her real one would probably not have anywhere near the budget this one did. The first major hitch occurred when Grace's "fiancé"—a senior named BJ, who called her "honey" and "darling" and "lover girl" in the school hallways—failed to come through with his guest list as instructed. Grace fretted for several evenings, checking e-mail hourly. At last, it was the night before their Friday presentation, and still no guest list. A lover's quarrel ensued. "Well, Grace," I said, "this is probably the most realistic part of the whole experience." Her frustration seemed somewhat universal: the girls thrived on this assignment; the boys barely tolerated it.

Each couple's baby was to appear at school on Monday. Baby weights and genders were picked out of a hat, and students were required to fashion an infant to weigh within one pound of the stated birth weight. "I hope BJ doesn't have big ideas about how to make our baby," Grace fretted.

"Oh, I don't think you have much to worry about there," I answered, certain that there wasn't a boy in the whole class who cared what his baby was made out of.

Soon Grace was stuffing nine pounds of rice into cut-up pant-yhose legs and making a somewhat realistic but very heavy ersatz baby girl. "Here, Mom," she said, handing it to me. "Would you like to hold your first grandchild?" Now it was time to fret about a name. What if BJ didn't like either of the girls' names Grace had picked? Again, I could reassure her with utmost confidence that there probably wasn't a boy in the class who would bat an eyelash no matter what his wife wanted to name the baby: Sarah, Emily, Cynthia, Pooh Bear, Dodo Brain—I was pretty sure it would be all the same to them. While Grace (and, theoretically, BJ) got a taste of parental responsibility for the next two weeks, I enjoyed being grandma to a bag of rice and never declined an opportunity to babysit. She was an exceedingly good baby who never even let out a whimper.

Chapter 10

That fall, Grace had a driver's license. Between school, jobs, and extracurricular activities, we didn't see much of our high schoolers. They were young women now, a fact they mentioned frequently—especially when I hung a list of their chores on the fridge door, asked if they had brushed their teeth, wrote their names on their lunch bags, or otherwise "treated them like ten-year-olds." They were enjoying their newfound independence; in fact, some weekends, the family car was hardly home at all. "It's time you and I went out on a date," Bob told me one day. "I'll ask Grace if we can use the van this weekend."

Though Rose and Brenda were only a year apart, Rose had a quiet, self-sufficient maturity about her and spent most of her free time in her room. Brenda seemed to be the only little girl in the house anymore. She still bounced, Tigger-like, through her days, running headlong—sometimes into things—and slapping dirty hands against the freshly painted walls of the hallway. Despite all she'd been through, she maintained a what-me-worry? demeanor, happy to be carefree and cared for, to remain young and childlike.

But for Bob and me, worry was anything but remote during the more-than-three-years' struggle, uncertainty, and expense related to Brenda's adoption. Even in the best of circumstances, international adoption is a complicated process; and an adoption like Brenda's, with all its anomalies, ground the gears of the system to a complete halt more than once. No sooner would we overcome one hurdle than another would loom up. The voluntary termination of parental rights was a long legal process, which was not in fact accomplished by those faxed documents we received in July. International complexities inherent in any such adoption were increased by Brenda's dubious legal status in the United States. We sent countless affidavits from our family doctors, school administrators, and pastors. Our friends and neighbors wrote references and testimonials. A state senator went to bat for us, but his letterhead did not impress the officials in Honduras. In time, we came to comprehend that there was no guarantee the adoption could be accomplished, and we feared at times we would have to send Brenda back. That was not what any of her three parents wanted, but bureaucracy operates mechanically, as responsive as a machine to emotions and extraordinary circumstances.

Brenda's adoption day. "Bam bam, she's yours!"

Though we tried to shield Brenda from our concerns, we hardly needed to; she never worried. To the extent that she knew of these difficulties, she viewed them as adult problems that the adults in her life would solve. Bob and I—the adults in her life—decided to cry uncle and hire an adoption attorney with a brilliant reputation, an extravagance we could afford only because of my grandmother's legacy. Through a few loopholes and some sleight of hand the seemingly impossible was accomplished, and the day finally came when the judge struck his gavel: Bam Bam. "She's yours." Brenda's adoption—though it was pulled off on a tenuous and tricky technicality—was irrefutably, unequivocally, incontrovertibly final. Then came the naturalization process—equally complicated, equally lengthy, and equally expensive. More high-priced attorneys, more obstacles, and more funds providentially provided just when we arrived at the end of our meager resources, and Brenda became a citizen of the United States of America.

Meanwhile, the mastermind of Brenda's makeover left Madison. When Dr. Hardy moved to Montana to establish a private practice, he left a gap not only in our lives but also in the Craniofacial Reconstructive Surgery Department at UW Hospital. Brenda was on hiatus, a break we all needed and enjoyed, until Dr. Hardy's successor arrived. The gentle giant, the casual, distracted, unassuming genius, was replaced by a compact powerhouse, a determined visionary who set goals, advocated for her patients, and would draw on every resource for Brenda's benefit.

Within a week of meeting Brenda, Dr. Mount ordered scans, assessed her situation, and plotted a series of surgeries that would correct many faults: a softball-sized hole in Brenda's skull; a misaligned, visibly crooked, and dysfunctional jaw; and damage to the chest wall and breast tissue which resulted when the truck that struck Brenda dragged her down the road in Trujillo. Little did we know then that the route Dr. Mount had painstakingly mapped out would be plagued by complications, infections, and failures.

Dr. Mount's first major project was to patch the large hole in Brenda's skull with a material she called "synthetic bone." Not only would this procedure improve the contours of Brenda's forehead; it also offered hope that she would someday be able to participate in athletics, a world that had been closed to her. At school, she had spent most gym classes seated on the sidelines. Up until now, she had not been involved in any team sports. Karate had proved a poor substitute, not to mention the embarrassment of being the only one in the class who had to wear a helmet. A brief stint on the Flag Troop was not very satisfying for someone with Brenda's energy level and competitive spirit. I started to dream of cheering her on at soccer and basketball games, and longed for these new vistas to open up for her.

The one thing that gave me pause was the word *synthetic*. Brenda's body had seemed exceptionally reactive to synthetic materials in the past. The expanders placed under her scalp years earlier had irritated her skin, thinned it, and broken through. Vicryl, a common suture material, aggravated Brenda's surgical wounds, broke down her skin, and slowed the healing of her incisions; her surgeons no longer used it. I timidly expressed my reservations, but a mother's casual observations didn't stack up very well against the training and experience of Dr. Mount, MD, FACS, FAAP. She assured me that there was no record of even one patient rejecting this type of synthetic bone. It was absolutely safe, an exact replica of human bone, and completely innocuous to all Homo sapiens.

The surgery was done, and all seemed well at first. Brenda was pleased with the smooth and symmetrical appearance of her forehead. But a couple of months after the operation, she began to complain of head pain. When her skin became hot and swollen over the patched area, Dr. Mount put her on antibiotics immediately. The symptoms subsided but returned the next month and did not respond as well to antibiotics. Her incision line went from pink and sore to purple and blistered. One day, a small white shard emerged, and Dr. Mount identified it as a piece of the synthetic patch. This situation continued throughout the postoperative months: Brenda's forehead periodically swelled, turned purple, blistered, and spit out synthetic bone in bits and pieces. Dr. Mount performed a few minor operations to clean the area and make adjustments, but to no avail. The sixth and final surgery in this unforeseen series—to remove all the remaining synthetic bone (in other words, to undo the entire effort)—was a bitter pill for all of us to swallow.

However, the indomitable Dr. Mount soon proposed Plan B. She and a neurosurgeon had conceived a way to repair Brenda's skull without relying on synthetic material. After allowing a rest period for her forehead to "settle down," they would collaborate on a cranioplasty, making an ear-to-ear incision over the crown of her head and using a graft from Brenda's own skull to patch the large hole in her forehead. I pictured the two doctors in my mind's eye, bent over Brenda's scans, devising a procedure so similar to our recent, heartbreaking failure that it was difficult to even listen to Dr. Mount's proposal, much less muster any enthusiasm for it.

But Dr. Mount was not dissuaded. While giving us a few months to think it over, she would tackle Brenda's jaw problems, which had never really been solved despite three rebuilds during her years with us, and at least one prior to that, in Honduras. Each reconstructive procedure had given relief for a while, but despite all our efforts, the joint would freeze up again over time. Besides the obvious problem—difficulty chewing and eating—Brenda's frozen jaw caused almost daily headaches which were aggravated by everyday activities such as practicing her clarinet, running, jumping, or doing therapy. Dr. Mount had consulted with a colleague from New York; and they planned to collaborate in surgery, using Brenda's own bone and cartilage, harvested from a rib, to craft a new joint. I was relieved that Dr. Mount was looking to Brenda's own body as the source of material for future reconstructions. The first thing she said as she spread the CAT scans out in front of us was, "No more synthetic material for Brenda. Her body doesn't like it."

That March, when Brenda was twelve years old, her fourth jaw reconstruction began—an ordeal we knew well and dreaded, even while we looked forward to the results. After taking children to surgery at least sixty times, I knew that procedures involving the mouth were some of the most miserable postoperatively, and this surgery was no exception. In the hours following the five-hour operation, Brenda lay in misery, nauseated and dizzy, with stitches both inside and outside her mouth, numbness throughout the right side of her face, an extremely dry mouth and considerable swelling. She could hardly communicate; any attempts at speech were unintelligible. I encouraged her to use hand signals, as nurses asked her regularly to rate her pain on a scale of one to five, medicating her with morphine accordingly. "Zero means no pain at all, and five means the worst pain you can think of," the nurse would repeat each time. "What number would you give your pain right now?"

By late that night, Brenda's nausea had passed, and her pain seemed tolerable. When asked to rate her pain, she would hold up just one or two fingers. Since she was in the Intensive Care Unit, with about sixteen medical professionals at a station only a few yards from her bed, I felt it was safe to go home for the night, and I began my goodbyes. As I leaned over to kiss her, I saw four fingers go up. "Oh, darn, Brenda," I said. "Are you up to four again? Should I ask for some morphine?" Brenda waved away my concern about pain and again put up four fingers, this time with more emphasis. She tried to speak, but I couldn't decipher her barely audible mumbling. I put my ear next to her mouth, and she repeated her muffled statement. At last, on the fourth or fifth try, I understood what she was saying: "You're parked on Level 4." The incapacitated Brenda, who needed not only constant but *intensive* care, continued to care for her mother through it all.

Brenda was soon home and back into the therapy schedule we knew so well. Every weekday, I took her for a session at the hospital. She was a passive participant while for an hour her therapists gently manipulated her jaw, took measurements, manipulated some more, and measured some more. She also received massage to help drain pockets of fluid that had developed in her jaw and neck. When I expressed concern about these subcutaneous puddles, which she had never had before, I was assured they were normal and contained only clear benign serum which her body would eventually reabsorb. One such pocket, right in front of her ear, would go squish-squish-squish whenever she ate, and even more so as her diet advanced to soft chewables like bread and canned tuna—a relief after ten days of pudding, yogurt, porridge, and pureed soup.

All was well for the first two weeks after surgery; but then Brenda developed swelling, pain, and drainage near her surgical incision. One, two, and then three antibiotics made no lasting change. There's no good time for an infection, but this was an especially bad time because she was at the point where aggressive therapy must be done to prevent scar tissue from forming and having its way with the healing tissues. Brenda's therapists were frustrated because the infection and slow healing impeded their efforts. Worse, Bob and I began having flashbacks to eighteen months prior, when Brenda's previous infection set in—the one that ultimately undid the reconstruction of her forehead.

No matter what happened, therapy must go on, so even while Brenda's infection was barely controlled, our relentless war on scar tissue continued with daily therapy at the hospital and at home. At a routine appointment one morning, Brenda's therapist expressed barely concealed alarm about the worsening condition of the area around Brenda's reconstructed jaw joint. The plastics department was called in and diagnosed an abscess that must be drained and irrigated as soon as possible. Brenda was immediately admitted as an inpatient.

Since Dr. Mount was laid up with a back injury, Brenda would have the services of Dr. Benz, head of the Plastics Department. His involvement was presented as quite an honor, but with the honor came a long wait for surgery—until about 8:30 that night. Brenda could not eat or drink the whole day but appeared happily forgetful of that fact as she caught up on her favorite movies from the pediatrics video library. The university medical system had succeeded so thoroughly in making hospitalization fun that when Brenda heard the word *admission* (an all-too-frequent occurrence), she thought, *TV, movies, computer games.* And as a frequent guest, well-known to the pediatrics department, she relished her reputation as a quick-witted young quipster. While a resident examined her that afternoon, he sat beside her on the bed. "I need to warn you, Brenda, that I'm going to touch the part of your face that's infected," he said kindly, "and it might hurt a little."

Brenda turned toward him. "I need to warn you," she said with a twinkle in her eye, "that I know karate, and it might hurt a little."

The long-awaited procedure was quickly done, and soon Brenda was back in her hospital room. We had seen repeatedly after surgeries that still waters run deep, as the seemingly unconscious Brenda heard and processed every conversation, sometimes contributing in unexpected ways. That night, Brenda lay quietly in her bed, breathing deeply in a morphine-induced sleep, as I called home to report on her surgery. While conversing with Bob, I was filling out a form required for free parking in the hospital ramp. I asked him, "Do you know offhand the license-plate number of our van?" "Hmmm," he said, "let me think." Before he could come up with it, the answer came from the apparently unconscious Brenda: "8-2-5-C-K-T."

But even the surprising antics of Brenda could not balance the grim news Dr. Benz delivered later that evening. The bone graft was in poor shape, invaded and weakened by infection. The cartilage was completely destroyed, and the doctor had to remove an 8-millimeter length of solid bone which had died and was flaking away. He would keep Brenda in the hospital until the weekend. He had taken cultures of the infected area, he explained, and some of them would require several days to grow out. Once the offending organism was identified, the infection could be targeted with the most suitable intravenous medicine. "The choice of antibiotic is based on the culture," he explained.

"I'm Hispanic," the seemingly unconscious Brenda piped up.

Of course, Brenda knew nothing of bacterial cultures, though she certainly was hospitable to them. A week later, she was still in the hospital while doctors puzzled over her inability to resist the infection that was plaguing her. The cultures taken during surgery showed nothing but a common and benign form of staph. "You see staph, and you prescribe oral Augmentin, and the patient gets better," the surgeon explained. "But Brenda doesn't get better. It's like adding two and two and not getting four." I began to feel a little desperate. This accursed infection was threatening a project in which many of us had invested heavily—not least, Brenda herself. I envisioned Dr. Mount's priceless piece of handiwork being removed, a few millimeters at a time, as the infection did its dirty work.

The next day, we were told that the bone cultures taken in surgery (still considered negative one day prior) had at last coughed up their secrets and grown out six different organisms. So Brenda had a stubborn bone infection (or six stubborn bone infections, depending how you looked at it) in her graft. She would undergo a procedure to insert a PICC line—a catheter inside a vein leading to her heart—which would allow for safe delivery of powerful antibiotics. I was sorry she would have to go through yet another procedure, but at last, they were getting out the heavy ammo, and that made me hopeful.

She was in her usual jocular mood while waiting and being prepped for the PICC line procedure. As the anesthesiologist bent over her, he asked in a mechanical way whether she'd had any breakfast. This was the fourth or fifth time anesthesiology residents and nurses had asked this, and Brenda was ready for a little fun.

"Yup," she answered.

The anesthesiologist's head popped up from his task. "What did you eat?" he asked in a concerned tone.

"Air," she answered.

No matter what happened, therapy must go on, and Brenda's therapists were relentless in their efforts to salvage the reconstructed joint. Each day, they spent at least an hour gently massaging and manipulating her jaw. Dr. Doyle would occasionally stop in during therapy sessions to monitor Brenda's progress. Over our several years' acquaintance, I had come to know this seasoned oral surgeon as a large, commanding man with a crusty exterior but a marshmallow interior. I enjoyed our conversations. Though he wasn't an infectious disease expert, I wanted his opinion on a theory I had formulated, so I caught him one day as he was leaving Brenda's therapy cubicle. I launched into a fairly detailed question about the possibility that Brenda's infection might be caused by bacteria picked up from the dung-infested soil of the road in Honduras where her accident had occurred. Was it possible that such bacteria could have invaded her rib when it was laid bare by her severe road burns and then lain dormant until the rib was harvested for a bone graft last month?

"Hmmm…" Dr. Doyle rubbed his chin thoughtfully, his other hand resting on the doorknob for several moments. He slowly opened the door while I awaited his expert response.

"Ya got my ass," he said and walked out, closing the door behind him.

In the midst of her long hospitalization, Brenda made a happy discovery. One day, when the nurse was taking her supper order and asked what she'd like to drink, Brenda jokingly answered, "Oh, just have them send up a six-pack of Pepsi." The nurse indeed wrote down "a six-pack of Pepsi." The kitchen indeed sent "a six-pack of Pepsi." So Brenda did a repeat performance the next day and received another six-pack of Pepsi. Brenda's love for Pepsi is legendary and is not the least diminished by the fact that it was a Pepsi delivery truck which ran her down in Honduras and started the whole chain of unfortunate events.

Chapter 11

W̲e were all eager for Brenda to come home. But once she did, the demands of her care were relentless. I was her adjunct case manager, therapist, nurse, driver, and tutor. She received two types of intravenous antibiotic at home; doses were administered every six hours and took about an hour to infuse. We did at-home therapy several times a day, in addition to daily therapy appointments at the hospital. We also made frequent visits to her surgeon and infectious disease doctors, who were monitoring her recovery. Between appointments, Brenda made brief visits to school. We were both sleep deprived because of nighttime medication doses. In her case, grades were suffering. In my case, the family was suffering, because if Mama ain't happy, ain't nobody happy. I got weird and weepy. Even though I'm not usually emotional, everything made me want to cry: being told I'd brought Brenda to the wrong clinic and our imminent appointment was actually on the other side of town; seeing the buds blooming on my geranium in the window; discovering that while we were gone to an appointment the dog threw up on the rug—whether good or bad, it all brought tears to my eyes and turbulence to my spirit.

It was easy to get completely caught up in medical world and miss the joys of spring unfolding around me. Nothing was further from my mind than asparagus, but one day. I noticed mature specimens of the perennial in my garden, several inches tall and ready for harvest. We had only two productive hills, which made each tender spear a treasure. As I reached down to cut a spear at its base, the knife slipped and sliced off the bud of a nearby shoot. Angry with myself, I launched into mock crying: "Waa-aaa-aaa-aaa-aaa…" Just then, I heard a noise behind me and turned to find a lawn-maintenance man on the other side of the fence, looking at me with concern while spraying the neighbor's grass. Embarrassed, I stood up and shrugged. Equally embarrassed, he looked away. "I bet you never heard asparagus cry before," I quipped.

As the spring months flew by, Kate was preparing to fledge. With high school graduation approaching, she got a summer job at a camp in Michigan. Anne, a cousin who had worked at the same camp, gave me a piece of advice to pass along to Kate: Take lots of warm clothes because June can be very cool at Camp Tall Turf. The next morning, Kate got up on the wrong side of the bed and was not very receptive to Anne's pearl of wisdom. "Anne went to a thrift store," I mentioned, a subtle tone of suggestion in my voice. "She bought a bunch of grungy clothes she didn't care about and took them to camp."

Kate glared at me over her cup of coffee. "Mom, I already have a bunch of grungy clothes I don't care about," she replied. "It's called my wardrobe."

At long last, Brenda had her final dose of intravenous medicines and began two months of oral antibiotics. Even though this milestone called for a celebration, we were too tired to party, so we slept in instead. It was the first time since Brenda's hospitalization that either of us had slept for more than five hours at a stretch. Since there was no test to assure us that the infection was gone, we could only hope and pray for the best while also watching for symptoms. We were relieved of our home nursing duties and the shelves of related medical supplies—but not the niggling anxiety at the back of our minds.

Besides that ever-present worry, my relationship with Brenda had taken a turn for the worse during the months of her illness. After she returned to school that spring, she often came home in a sullen mood. "What's wrong, Brenda? Did something happen at school today?" I might ask.

"Oh, man, you don't know the half of it," was a typical answer. But when I tried to explore the problem, Brenda would claim that (1) she didn't want to talk about it, (2) I wouldn't be able to do anything about it anyway, and/or (3) it was way too complicated to go into. She wanted little to do with me at home, spending most of her time with earphones on or in her room. When she must sit beside me at church, she turned her back toward me and placed a stack of Bibles and songbooks between us. Sometimes, when she was particularly distant, I imagined that she was fantasizing about life with her birth-mother, Sonia, on the idyllic beaches of Trujillo. She had much to deal with. Not only did she have two mothers and all the conflicted feelings that must go with that. She was also thirteen and in middle school, a difficult time even in the best of circumstances. The boys spit on her notebooks and were a general annoyance. And the girls were into boys and makeup, both of which must have created some awkwardness for Brenda. As she grew up, she was becoming more and more self-conscious about her appearance; she did not venture confidently into new settings as she used to.

I remembered an incident from my own coming-of-age, a phase of life I navigated in the most awkward way possible. All through grade school, I had often worn my hair in pigtails, as many girls did. Then when I was in sixth grade, a boy in the desk behind mine called attention to a small scar on the back of my scalp, the result of a fall when I was a young child. After my classmate pointed out this imperfection, I never wore pigtails again, instead hiding the tiny flaw with my long blonde hair. I must remember that when I thought about Brenda.

Meanwhile, Dr. Mount began anticipating Brenda's next operation. Because one side had been crushed in the accident, her jaw-line was quite visibly lopsided, a fact that had never been addressed during previous joint reconstructions. The surgeon devised a scheme for straightening it, which would improve both appearance and function. She planned to cut Brenda's jaw in half at the chin and install a device that would extend the short side, bringing the top and bottom into better alignment. I'm not sure why this proposed procedure sounded so barbaric after all that had already been done in Brenda's previous thirty-five operations, but suddenly, I was weary of all this. I felt bad for Brenda and wondered whether it was good for her, to keep busting her up and putting her back together, not to mention risking one infection after another. Brenda was eager to cooperate with whatever Dr. Mount proposed, but that gave me pause as well. I worried that as Brenda grew older and more self-aware, she might be motivated by the hope that if she just had enough operations, she would finally look normal. However realistic or fanciful her expectations, I did not want her to remember or perceive me as an obstacle to whatever improvement might be made in her appearance.

I wouldn't be completely honest if I didn't admit that I sometimes wondered what drove Brenda's surgeons. I had the greatest confidence in Dr. Mount, and I admired her courage. She wanted the best for Brenda and had not given up on her dream of repairing her forehead, jaw, and chest, despite all the setbacks. But I could also imagine how hard it might be to stop once you got started on a challenging and unique case. Over the years, I had watched surgeons sizing up our foster children's disfigured faces from every angle, like sculptors looking critically at an unfinished work of art. If only they could shave off some scar tissue here and trowel on a bit of bone there. But when a surgeon wants to take your child's head apart and find an improved way of reassembling it, it gives a parent pause. And I knew from prior surgeons' comments that everything on the damaged side of Brenda's head was knocked askew. Trying to chart a route through her cranial anatomy was like trying to navigate California using a roadmap of Angola. In any case, one thing was clear: the doctors would keep tweaking and tweaking until we cried uncle.

Graduation weekend provided distraction from these concerns and the constant static they created in the background of my mind. The week was a whirlwind of activity—grandparents' arrival from out of town, Rose's eighth-grade banquet on Thursday, Rose's graduation on Saturday, a celebratory family dinner that night, church and Kate's high school graduation on Sunday, and then Kate's party on Monday, Memorial Day. At some point early Tuesday morning, while we chatted over mugs of coffee and basked in the memories of the weekend's festivities, we realized that Kate had to leave that day for her summer-camp job in Michigan. Her departure just a couple of hours later came like a cold shower for all of us. She hurriedly packed her bags and threw them into the back of the van. As she and Bob pulled out of the driveway for the six-hour trip, the rest of us gathered on the front porch. "Goodbye, Kate!" we called, waving cheerily as though she were leaving for a sleepover and not the whole summer. As if it were just a temporary departure, and not the Big Leaving, the Leaving at the End of High School, when one goes away and doesn't come back. I went back inside and walked through the residue of Kate's party: cards, giftwrap, napkins, and paper cups still scattered about the house. It seemed as though she would be back by suppertime—not as though she had just gone out into the world to seek her fortune.

Thus our first set of daughters was gone. Though all five were born within eight years, we had, in a way, two families: our older three who arrived within twenty-three months; and our other two, both of whom joined our family years later, after their infancies were over, at ages two and six respectively, and were a year apart in age. Suddenly, Bob, Rose, Brenda, and I seemed to be rambling around in a half-empty house. On one hand, this transition felt right and timely. Bob and I had anticipated our children's departures for decades, with a mixture of apprehension and eagerness. We had prepared our kids for life away from us, and now that they were ready, we should feel pride and not grief.

I should celebrate my newfound freedom. I should enjoy grocery shopping with just one cart, like normal people. I should appreciate whole days without even one load of laundry. I should relish the peace and quiet. But there was no denying that grief was bedfellow to my sense of accomplishment. I felt a mixture of satisfaction and desolation. The culmination of a job well done and the loneliness of three empty chairs at the table. Mourning is never a one-time act but must be repeated in a thousand increments as new facets of loss reveal themselves. *I might as well close the piano so the keys don't gather dust. I've got to stop buying so many bananas. I guess I'll put Kate's mug away so it doesn't get broken.* Such simple observations brought twinges of sadness and loss—feelings that I shook off by recalling some comical story from our hectic happy years or finding a new recipe to try for supper. Sometimes during a long, quiet evening, I would imagine that I could hear the laughter that had soaked into the walls during those many chatty, giggly dinners over twenty years' time at our trestle table.

Then suddenly there was the joy of our children's return for the holidays. Our faraway daughters seemed to come in on a breeze of fresh energy and hilarity. Mealtimes were once again boisterous affairs, as youthful, feminine gaiety filled the house. Bob and I basked in the refreshing levity of our daughters' giggles, reminiscing, and fun. Their occasional shout-downs brought back memories of past years, but I felt no obligation to rein them in. If they hadn't learned good table manners by now, I'd just come to dinner with earplugs.

Kate came home from college a vegetarian. Though I prefer that my children be at peace with food, I took the same approach I had always taken to dietary hang-ups and dislikes. Put plenty of varied items on the table; if someone's taste buds or ethics could not reconcile with a certain food, she did not have to eat it. One afternoon during the holidays, I decided to roast a chicken. This turned into a full-course dinner: mashed potatoes, gravy, corn, rolls. When I took the chicken out of the oven, it looked so lovely—delicately browned with crispy skin—that I decided to put it on a platter and serve it whole, like in that famous Norman Rockwell painting. I wasn't trying to aggravate anyone's sensibilities, but without thinking, I set the bird right in front of Kate. "I'm sorry, Mother," she said, looking askance at our main dish, "but I cannot eat dinner with that dead animal on the table."

Before long and not surprisingly, our daughters were engaged in an animated discussion of meat eating, and we got onto the subject of beef tongue. "I can't believe anyone would ever eat tongue," Kate ranted. "That's the grossest food I've ever heard of!" Naturally, she was not happy to hear that when she was small and tongue was a cheap cut of meat, she ate it somewhat regularly. In fact, she was indignant: "How could you feed me that!?" she cried.

Eventually, the conversation moved on to a different topic, but Rose remained quiet and thoughtful. At last, her ponderings emerged. "Mom, how long can a cow live without its tongue, anyway?" she asked.

The very social Brenda thoroughly enjoyed her older sisters' visit and lapsed into lonely boredom when they left. Whole hours passed quietly, and we all enjoyed it except for Brenda, who declared us the most boring family in Madison. After she threw herself into a chair for the fourth time in one afternoon, with her oft-repeated cry, "I don't know what to do with myself," I decided to float an idea or two. Rather than my usual answer ("Do I look like an activities director?"), I suggested that she walk to the neighborhood library for some books or a movie. "That's the dumbest library in Madison," she answered. "I've read every book and seen every movie they have in that dump." Taking pity on the poor child, I offered to drive her to a large branch library in a different part of town. Brenda agreed grudgingly, but Rose jumped at the chance. (Brenda read out of desperation; Rose read because it's FUN!) After an hour of browsing, I had an armload of books, and Brenda was similarly burdened, though I looked askance at her selections. Offered a wide array of classic and high-quality teen literature, she always came away with the same: paperback fiction, teen romance, and maudlin cancer novels. She wasn't interested in *Anne of Green Gables*, *Jane Eyre*, or *Little Women* because "Books that happened in the olden days are dumb."

Rose, surprisingly, emerged with the lowest number of books: one. It was a very thick hardback. "What have you got there?" I asked.

"A biography of Leonard Bernstein," she answered.

The quiet, thoughtful Rose slipped easily back into her routine and seemed relieved that the boisterous busyness of the holidays was over. One of the supposed benefits of adopting Brenda was that Rose would have a sister close in age, a companion for the "lonely" years after the older girls left home. Now that those years were here, Rose had almost no interest in Brenda's companionship. Rose was a bookish child and a serious A+ student who studied hard, practiced her flute faithfully, and enjoyed solitude.

Brenda, on the other hand, was 100% social and completely incapable of entertaining herself. She asked me nightly to play *family* board games (big emphasis on the word *family*) and was disappointed when I declined in favor of reading or getting to some work I had to do. With a sigh, she might go dig up a book (ho hum) and sit near me, but companionable silence was not in her repertoire. "Would you say my head is a weird shape?" she might ask. Or "Cassandra says I should start shaving my legs. What do you think?" Rose was always careful to read or study in her room, thus avoiding the pestering interruptions of her little sister. One of Rose's few faults was that she sometimes took the part of the smug, superior older sister. One afternoon, I heard Rose demanding an apology for some perceived misdeed on Brenda's part. "Love means never having to say you're sorry, Rose," Brenda stated with grave certainty. "It's in the Bible."

During one of those quiet dinnertimes while we were readjusting to the absence of our three college-age daughters, Rose, ever the serious and forward-thinking young woman, pondered aloud the value which would accrue on a certificate of deposit she had taken out the previous fall. "It's worth $500 now, and in five years, it'll be worth just under $600," she commented. "That's a gain of less than twenty percent. That doesn't seem like the greatest investment." Bob assured her that as a college-bound fifteen-year-old, she was making good use of summer earnings while avoiding the dangers of riskier investments.

Thirteen-year-old Brenda, who up until now had shown a great deal more interest in buttering her roll than in this conversation, suddenly spoke up. "By the way, is somebody saving for my college education?" she asked around a bite of food. "Because I'm not."

Chapter 12

‡

In January, Brenda and I met with Dr. Mount to discuss the skull graft she had spoken of so often. As we entered her office, her question, "Would you like to see your scans?" put me in mind of the classic come-on, "Would you like to see my etchings?" I went into the meeting prepared to resist a hard sell. Of course, I didn't want to subject Brenda to another skull surgery, after the disastrous failure of the previous attempt. But the difference in Dr. Mount's current proposal—and I hoped it would be a significant one—was that this time it would be done entirely with native tissue. Since our skulls have two layers of bone with space in between, Dr. Mount and a neurosurgeon would be able to remove a section of skull and flay off one layer to use as a patch over the hole in Brenda's forehead. It would be a big operation, requiring up to two weeks in the hospital.

We listened quietly as Dr. Mount pitched the planned operation and drew lines in wax pencil on a plastic model that bore little resemblance to Brenda's damaged skull. In between answers to my skeptical questions, she made empowering statements to Brenda. "This is entirely up to you," she stated emphatically. "You're in the driver's seat." I could hardly face the prospect of such a major operation, and even the courageous Brenda, feeling a little more empowered than she wanted to be, admitted that the weight of the decision was making her nervous. As if I were dealing with a pushy car salesman and not a world-class craniofacial reconstruction specialist, I stood, put on my coat, grasped Brenda's hand, and said, "We'll just think about this over the weekend."

As we headed home, there was no cheerful chatter from the subdued Brenda about hospital menu selections, free Pepsi six-packs, or the vast video library in the pediatric unit. Was it just this one operation that was giving her pause? Or was she growing into a pained awareness that despite many procedures past and future, her appearance would never be normal? I wanted to give her the freedom to say no. I wanted to assure her that she would always be beautiful to us, whether she had twenty more operations or none.

Little did we know that the decision would be made for us. Dr. Mount called a few days later to report that after further consultation with a cohort of experts, she had opted to put the skull repair on hold. I wondered what had in fact swayed her: the opinions of her peers or Brenda's and my hesitation. (That skull surgery would indeed be done eventually to relieve chronic, debilitating headaches, but not until Brenda was in her twenties.) For the immediate future, Dr. Mount suggested the jaw-lengthening process she had proposed earlier. This would require an initial operation to break Brenda's jaw and install a distractor—a device which would elongate her jawbone on the damaged side of her face by stimulating her body to lay down new bone, a process called osteogenesis. Once the jaw was adequately lengthened, the device would be removed. The cutting and breaking of bones, and the multiple surgeries this process would require, were painful to contemplate. And so was the chance of failure. Several surgeries must succeed for this reconstructive effort to work, and how likely was that in Brenda's case? But I was resolute in my desire to be supportive. If Brenda opted to go through with it, I would stand behind her, or beside her, or lie in bed next to her holding the emesis basin.

As the date of the first bone-lengthening surgery neared, I convinced myself that my fears were probably unfounded. But only a few hours after the operation, my apprehensions were realized. A complication would not only keep Brenda hospitalized for several extra days; it might stall out the whole project. While cutting through the bone of Brenda's lower jaw, Dr. Mount had inadvertently nipped the roots of a molar. The tooth popped out of its socket and lay beside Brenda's jawbone, barely attached to her gum by a couple strands of skin.

That tooth was the subject of great consternation and, I'm quite certain, a few sleepless nights for Dr. Mount. After two scans and much deliberation, the experts decided that the tooth must go, in part because it posed a risk of infection, which we knew from Brenda's history was always a concern. The tooth was removed a few days later, in surgery, under general anesthesia. Though taking Brenda to the operating room in order to cut a couple strands of skin seemed like making a mountain out of a molar, I appreciated Dr. Mount's desire to cause her the least pain and trauma possible. Because the tooth's dislocation created a weak point in Brenda's jaw-bone, the bone-lengthening process would be delayed but only for two weeks.

Brenda forgave Dr. Mount's slipup immediately and went into her tooth-removal surgery with even more than the usual pluck, just so her doctor wouldn't feel so bad. A couple of weeks later, when osteogenesis began, she faced it with the same courage. To force new bone growth, the severed ends of her lower jaw had to be prevented from growing back together. To get a sense of how this felt, imagine taking two raw bone ends which are just beginning to mend and forcing them apart over and over, using a small metal key to turn screws inserted into them. Oxycodone was helpful but still… ouch.

When the active bone lengthening was finished, Brenda resumed painful therapy to regain the mobility lost since her surgery. After a month of "neglect," her jaw could not open far enough to eat even a small grape. But the joint quickly loosened up again, and she was so pleased with her improved appearance that she endured therapy willingly. Dr. Mount was ecstatic with the outcome. When it was finished, she gazed with utmost satisfaction at Brenda's scans. "These are the most beautiful photos I've ever seen!" she crowed.

"Can I have those?" Brenda asked.

"No way!" Dr. Mount answered. "I'm taking these with me everywhere I go. I'm sleeping with them under my pillow. When I get a bout of insomnia or wake up worried about something, I'll just flick on the light, hold up these scans, and say, 'See? At last I did a successful surgery on this child!'"

About six months after it was installed, the bone-lengthening hardware was removed in surgery, at which time Dr. Mount broke

111

and realigned Brenda's upper jaw. Brenda had some hard days after that; her jaw was busted up again, and she was in a lot of pain. She declared this the worst surgery she had ever had. Since the surgeon again had to cut through the accursed scar tissue in her jaw, she lost the mobility we had worked so hard for and was back to square one, facing aggressive therapy to restore it. The good news is that the surgery made a noticeable difference in both function and appearance, adding 7 millimeters to the width of her upper jaw and improving the alignment of her upper and lower jaws and teeth. It was a long, slow recovery which included lots of pain, poor appetite ("It's too much work to eat."), and anemia.

A week after the operation, we went to a postoperative checkup that unexpectedly turned into a three-hour odyssey of procedures and tests. After we returned home, the exhausted Brenda curled up with a book while I sat at the computer nearby. After a long period of quiet, she asked, seemingly out of nowhere, "Am I curable?"

Assuming that she must be mulling over that day's diagnosis of anemia, I said, "Oh yeah. Anemia is easy to fix in a healthy young person like you."

"No," she said. "I mean, am *I* curable?" That's how she asked it. That's how she asked whether she would ever look normal. Whether people would ever stop staring at her. Whether her surgeons would ever stop tweaking. Whether she would find peace with her own appearance. That's how she asked it.

I turned away from the computer screen to face her. "What do you mean?"

"Will I ever not have to have surgery anymore?" she asked.

Of course, I told her, she could stop having surgery any time she wanted.

But how long did I think it would be, she wanted to know, until she would look normal and wouldn't need any more operations?

"Well, Brenda," I replied, sitting beside her and enfolding her in my arms, "I don't think you'll ever look as if no accident happened to you. But I do think that sometime you're going to say, 'Hey, I can live with this. I'm content with the way I look.'"

She replied with a heavy sigh. I didn't know whether I had said the right thing. I did know I was expressing more hope than conviction.

But at some point, or probably at many points over a period of years, Brenda found peace with her appearance, and her long sequence of reconstructive surgeries came to an end. She turned to face the world and her future with confidence, resolved to ignore curious stares and whispered comments. She and her sisters sometimes did postmortems on awkward moments and insensitive questions. For instance, when Brenda recounted how a woman had unabashedly stared at her in a store and asked, "What happened to your *face*?" her sisters suggested the retort, "What happened to your *manners*?" Then they all burst into laughter. Although there was a certain comfort in her sisters' sympathy, Brenda never in fact responded to tactless questions or comments in kind.

Brenda as a high school senior, with her parents

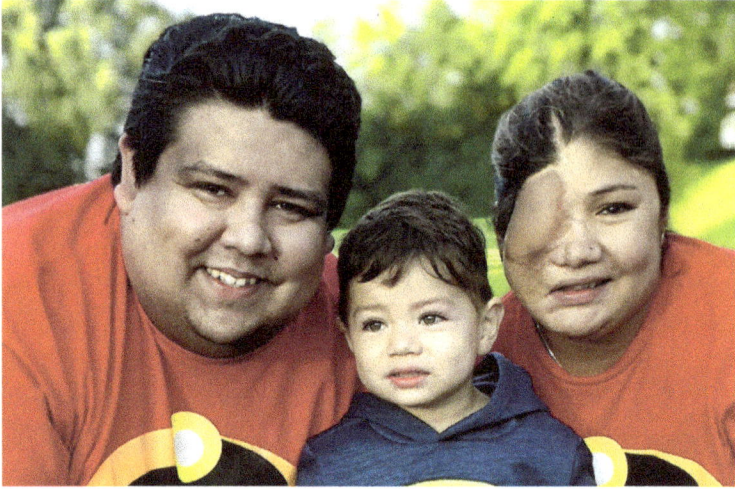

And today, with her own family, husband Mario and son Elías

And she never did settle on one name either. She's gone by Brenda, Evelyn, Evie, and even Brevie. She's lived out the meanings of her names, daily expressing light, life, persistence, and courage. When someone else's hope wanes, she generously shares from her own supply and the depth of her experience. She gives solace and encouragement to her patients. She is a source of warmth and caring when their spark of life is at its ebb.

It wasn't until Brenda was grown up and I looked back over her life with us that I realized the breadth and weight of her accomplishments. By the age of six, she had survived a horrible, disfiguring accident and moved to a strange country where she knew no one. She started a new life and learned a new language. She embraced seven strangers, adopting them as her family with hardly a backward glance. During her years with us, she underwent more than fifty surgeries, facing them with courage and good humor. She endured all kinds of pain but never pitied herself or became bitter, angry, or entitled. She maintained an adventuresome, curious, friendly, and forgiving spirit. She was and is kind, compassionate, generous, and good-humored. She is a stellar wife and a loving mother. She attained her goal to work in health care and has a fine reputation as a certified nursing assistant, currently employed at UW Hospital, her home away from home away from home.

While our daughter Kate was away at college, one of Brenda's favorite bands performed a concert on her campus. Kate ushered at the concert, in the hope of obtaining autographs from the band members for her younger sister back home. After the performance, Kate managed to get the autographs of one or two musicians, but the most prominent band members made haste to their bus, carrying a folding table between themselves and the crowd like a shield. Kate waited outside the bus, but it was soon apparent that they had stiff-armed their fans and wouldn't be reappearing. She kicked a tire angrily. "I just wanted to get your autographs for my sister!" she shouted. "If you knew her, you'd want *her* autograph!"

That is a fitting tribute to Brenda because however she might sign her name—Brenda, Evelyn, Evie, or Brevie—she is, in a profound way, a celebrity: a person and a life to be celebrated. And I do. Live long and prosper, my beloved daughter. God bless you.

> I don't think of all the misery, but
> of the beauty that still remains.
> —Anne Frank, *The Diary of a Young Girl*

CPSIA information can be obtained
at www.ICGtesting.com
Printed in the USA
JSHW021515231020
8998JS00005B/53

9 781648 013850